I NEVER CHEAT ON MY HUSBAND

Borgo Press Books by GEORGES FEYDEAU

I Never Cheat on My Husband

I NEVER CHEAT ON MY HUSBAND

A PLAY IN THREE ACTS

GEORGES FEYDEAU

Adapted and Translated by Frank J. Morlock

THE BORGO PRESS
MMXIII

I NEVER CHEAT ON MY HUSBAND

Copyright © 2002, 2013 by Frank J. Morlock

FIRST BORGO PRESS EDITION

Published by Wildside Press LLC

www.wildsidebooks.com

DEDICATION

To Carmen

CONTENTS

CAST OF CHARACTERS 9
ACT I 11
ACT II 103
ACT III 189
ABOUT THE TRANSLATOR 237

CAST OF CHARACTERS

Gerard Saint Franquet

Des Saugettes

Plantaredi

Tommy

M. Giclefort

Mme. Giclefort

Manager (Godache)

Waiter (Lamiche)

Bellboy (Pointet)

Usher

Victor

Bichon

Micheline

Dotty Summerson

Maid (Sophy)

Servants

Tourists

Tennis Players

ACT I

Chatel-Sancy (Auvergne). Country landscape—hills. To the left—exterior of the "Modern Hotel." Three windows—to the right: The tennis courts—tables, chairs, gazebo between the hotel and the tennis courts. Before the curtain rises—the voices of tennis players: "Ready!" "Play!" "Your ball!" "Bravo!" "Your ball!" "Outside" "Oh damn—fifteen for us."

As the curtain rises, the Waiter is cleaning the table and dusting the chairs. The game continues in the tennis court. The Manager comes in from the hotel.

Manager (huffing and breathing hard, wiping his face)

Ahh! I'm just about dead. Hey, Lamiche, give me a hand.

Waiter

Yes, Mr. Godache— Oh, it really is rather hot.

Manager

I'm sweating, my friend, I'm sweating. There is no other word.

Waiter

It's ninety-six in the shade.

Manager

What a summer! It's a killer. They ask when it will rain. I was afraid of that, so I rushed to the station to be there on time.

Waiter

Didn't you have your watch?

Manager

Yes, only I didn't have the time. I have an excellent watch, only it wanders occasionally.

Waiter

Oh—

Manager

It doesn't vary a half minute a day. But, sometimes, it stops for an hour and then starts going again.

Waiter

That doesn't surprise me. I had a cousin like that. She had palpitations, then one day she passed away.

Manager

She went well.

Waiter

Yes.

Manager

Just like my watch. Let's get going. (pushing him) Go, go.

(At this moment, the Maid appears in the window, holding out a carpet. As the Manager goes in the hotel, she accidentally drops the rug and it lands on the Manager's head.)

Maid

Oh, pardon, sir.

Manager

Pay attention to what you're doing, Sophy. This is unacceptable.

Maid

It's the rug of Madame Plantaredi.

Manager

That doesn't make it any more agreeable to me. Suppose it fell on a guest—

Maid

Oh, I would have paid attention.

Manager

A charming thing to say to me.

Mme Giclefort (rushing out of the hotel, to Giclefort, who follows her)

Come, Jewel, come—you have the folding chairs and umbrellas?

Giclefort

I've got everything. (to Manager) Hello, Mr. Godache.

Mme Giclefort

Mr. Godache won't have lunch with me at the hotel today.

Manager

Madame is unfaithful to us.

Mme Giclefort (simpering)

Oh—it's not me. When I commit an infidelity, it's with a man. But still—as it is with me— (to Giclefort) Right, Benjamin?

Giclefort

Right, my dear.

Mme Giclefort

We will dine at la Rochemabelle.

Manager

Oh, oh— You will dine very badly.

Mme Giclefort

Yes—but there's a magnificent view.

Manager

Indeed. But it cannot be digested.

Giclefort

Happily, it won't stay longer.

Mme Giclefort

Oh! Oh! Charming— How witty he is! He talks like Courteline.

Manager

Then go, go to lunch at la Rochemabelle.

Giclefort

Indeed, yes—one time.

Manager

Funny idea— When here you can— But, you are on the pension here—you are not à la carte.

Mme Giclefort

No, no!

Manager

Ah yes, oh—good! Then things will be all right. You know, I

say that one dines badly at la Rochemabelle. After all, what do I know?

Giclefort

And then, we are in good company—and one can eat only a little.

Manager

Yes—like two lovers.

Giclefort

Eh, yes.

Mme Giclefort

Oh—the fact is! I don't know what is going on with Mr. Giclefort—maybe it's the effect of the water here. Truly, there are moments. (little amorous shiver) Ah—

Giclefort (with satisfaction)

I am in voice, yes, I am in voice.

Mme Giclefort (coughing, modest)

Hem!

Manager (to Giclefort)

What's all this?

Giclefort (to his wife)

Say, tell him a little bit about last night.

Mme Giclefort

Come! Come! You have no shame—at our age.

Giclefort

What's wrong with our age? We have seen sixty-six springtimes; but it's still springtime.

Mme Giclefort (simpering)

Go on! Go on!

Giclefort

And when I am sixty-six—I'm only sixty-five, Mme Giclefort is the elder. Me, I am the gigolo!

Mme Giclefort

Yes, well then, come Mr. Gigolo. Do you have your shawl?

Giclefort

I have my shawl—yes—but I am a gigolo. (very proudly) I am the gigolo.

(They leave by the right. Noise of brakes and bells in the distance.)

Manager

Oh—the bus from the hotel! (calling) Lamiche, Pointet.

A Voice

Here!

Manager (to the Bellboy who appears)

The bus, my boy.

Bellboy

Yes, sir, I heard it.

Waiter (to Bellboy)

Come, Pointet.

(Waiter and Bellboy leave by the back.)

Des Saugettes (running in from the right, to the Manager)

Good day, sir. I ask your pardon. Madame Plantaredi sends me to find a red silk scarf that she left in her room.

Manager

A silk?

Des Saugettes

Yes, you know, that she puts around her neck.

Manager

Yes— The Maid will know. (calling) Sophy.

Sophy (at the window)

Sir?

Manager

A silk scarf? Do you see a silk scarf?

Des Saugettes

Red?

Sophy

Red?

Des Saugettes

Yes.

Sophy

I am going to see.

Des Saugettes

If you please.

(Sophy disappears from the window.)

Des Saugettes (to Manager)

Thanks a lot.

Bichon (crossing the tennis net)

Sir.

Des Saugettes (astonished)

Me?

Bichon

Good day, sir.

Des Saugettes (still astonished)

Good day, miss.

Bichon (pointing to a ball outside the netting)

The ball, there!

Des Saugettes

Oh—pardon. (he gets it)

Bichon (taking the ball he hands to her)

If you please! Thanks.

Des Saugettes

Nothing at all. (to Manager) Who is that young girl?

Manager

She's a hooker!

Des Saugettes

Oh.

Manager

Sent by the government for the visit of the Shah of Persia.

Des Saugettes

Ah?

Sophy (returning to window)

Sir.

Manager and Des Saugettes

What?

Sophy

You're sure it's red?

Des Saugettes

Scarlet—or burgundy.

Sophy

I'll look again.

Manager (seeing tourists arrive)

Excuse me, more guests arriving.

Des Saugettes

Go right ahead.

Bellboy

This way, ladies and gentlemen.

Manager

You wish rooms, ladies and gentlemen?

Several

If you please. Dumb question.

Manager (to one of his employees)

My register.

First Guest

I want a separate dressing room.

Manager

Surely. You will get 15 or 19. And do you want a large bed or two beds?

Second Guest

Two! We are married.

Manager

Very well, very well. Number 14 for this gentleman and his wife. And you, sir? A big bed or two beds?

Lady Guest

But I don't know, sir.

Manager

Oh, excuse me, excuse me, I thought you were together.

Lady Guest

Huh?

Male Guest

No, no! Not yet!

Lady Guest (scandalized)

What do you mean, not yet?

(Saint Franquet enters and a tennis ball strikes him in the back. Bichon reappears in the back.)

Bichon

Did a ball fall here?

Saint Franquet

Exactly, Madame, on me.

Bichon

Oh, pardon, sir— Oh, Saint Franquet. (she comes around the net to him)

Saint Franquet

Bichon! (aside) Oh, hell!

Bichon

It's terrible that one cannot stay in some hole in the wall without meeting people one once knew—isn't it?

Saint Franquet

Just what I thought.

Bichon

It's not proper?

Saint Franquet

And—by what chance are you here?

Bichon

Oh, fine. I haven't told you, doll! It's true I have not seen you since—

Saint Franquet

Doll?

Bichon

Why not?

Saint Franquet

Good, good, I don't mind.

Bichon

I am no longer with Boutinot.

Saint Franquet

What?

Bichon

I jilted him (pause) 'cause he kicked me out.

Saint Franquet

No?

Bichon

Because of my hairdresser.

Saint Franquet

Oh!

Bichon

It wasn't my fault. He chose the hairdresser himself. The one who dressed his mother.

Saint Franquet

Oh—well then!

Bichon

Well then, indeed! That made it even worse. He couldn't stand it that a hairdresser— He was very snobbish, you know.

Female Tennis Player (appearing behind the net)

Well—Bichon?

Bichon

Right away! Right away! (the female Tennis Player disappears) (to Saint Franquet) We'll see each other a little bit, right?

Saint Franquet

Certainly.

Bichon

Since we've found each other here— The two of us. Ah! Heaven does funny things. I had a yen for you once, you know.

Saint Franquet

Can that be true?

Bichon (sitting on the bench)

When I think there was never anything between us—

Saint Franquet

Oh—you didn't want it.

Bichon

Why?

Saint Franquet

Boutinot was my friend.

Bichon

Well—he was mine, too.

Saint Franquet

It's true.

Bichon

You are the only one of his friends who didn't try.

Female Tennis Player (reappearing)

Well, Bichon—come on!

Bichon (rising)

Yes, yes, old girl, I'm coming. (to Saint Franquet) We are going to straighten that out, now, aren't we? All my days are free.

Saint Franquet

And the nights.

Bichon

Oh— They are taken.

Saint Franquet

Ah!

Bichon

Yes, I am attached to the Shah.

Saint Franquet

What do you mean by that?

Bichon

The Shah of Persia—! I am here for him! Yes, my dear! I seem like nothing of the sort. Well, I am the favorite. For twenty-one days— The time of the cure.

Saint Franquet

You don't say so.

Bichon

It's done the diplomatic way. The Consul spoke to Foreign Affairs, which spoke to the Interior, which, in turn, spoke to the Prefect—near Maxims. And I was the one chosen from all the others, as the youngest, the prettiest, and because I don't look like a whore.

Saint Franquet

My compliments.

Bichon (sitting down again)

So, you understand, naturally, my nights. Oh— They are not merely acts of being here—because the Shah, you know—phtt! He does it like a drunken lion brandishing a knife. But in bed— in love— Oh! No— between us—indeed—no!

Saint Franquet

Aha!

Bichon

Oh! No, no, no more of the Shah, no more of the Shah.

Male Tennis Player (against the net)

Well, Bichon— Are you playing or not?

Bichon (rising)

But, I'm coming. I'm coming. I'm talking with this gentleman. A friend. (presenting the player to Saint Franquet) Another.

Saint Franquet (bowing)

Sir!

Bichon (to Saint Franquet)

Then—soon.

Saint Franquet

Certainly.

Bichon (returning to him)

Moreover, I won't be irritated by talking to you.

Saint Franquet

To talk with me.

Bichon

It's the same thing. I have to talk to you, because you can give me some advice. It's about a thing proposed to me—a thing—important!

Saint Franquet (ruffling her)

Important.

Bichon

Don't joke—it is serious. They want me to go into the theater—

Saint Franquet

Aha!

Bichon

There, as you are a painter, it's the same as art. What should I take up? Singing or dancing girl?

Saint Franquet

Is that so? No, but— You sing, too?

Bichon

Well—in my fashion?

Tennis Player

Out of tune.

Bichon

"Out of tune."— There. The other one. He doesn't know how to return a tennis ball and he mixes in like a judge. No—that is to say, I sing well enough by myself— It's the accompaniment that puts me out.

Saint Franquet

Aha.

Bichon

You understand. The orchestra plays one tune, I sing another— we have to go together. Despite myself, I sing the same thing as the orchestra.

Saint Franquet

Oh—the devil! This is serious.

Bichon

Yes— Oh! But the director said it wasn't important, since I have very pretty legs.

Saint Franquet

Oh, then—

Female Tennis Player

Oh— Listen, Bichon, that's enough— It is boring.

Bichon

Coming, coming. (to Saint Franquet) See you again, Gerard. We will see each other.

Saint Franquet

Yes, yes.

Bichon

That's agreed. Soon! (crossing the net) Who do I serve to?

Female Tennis Player

You receive, little one, you receive.

Bichon

Oh—fine.

(They disappear. Saint Franquet watches them and makes a little pout of discontent.)

Usher

Here, the Manager, sir. (he disappears)

Manager (entering)

Excuse me, sir, but I had to take care of some guests who just arrived. Doubtless you wish a room?

Saint Franquet

Indeed—soon.

Manager

Would you give me your name?

Saint Franquet

Gerard Saint Franquet.

Manager

Oh—for sure.

Saint Franquet

You know me?

Manager

Not at all, sir.

Saint Franquet

Oh—you spoke as if—"For sure."

Manager

I cannot doubt what you tell me.

Saint Franquet

Certainly.

Des Saugettes (out of breath, brandishing a scarf)

There it is, sir, I got it.

Saint Franquet

Oh—I thank you very much, for returning to tell me.

Des Saugettes

Oh—I didn't return. I just had to come this way. I beg your pardon.

Saint Franquet

But go on. I would be desolated—

Des Saugettes

Good-day, sir. (he leaves by the right)

Saint Franquet

Communicative, that fellow.

Giclefort (rushes in, followed by his wife)

You wait for me, okay, you wait for me.

Mme Giclefort

Yes, go, sweety, go!

Giclefort (entering the hotel)

Right, right—

Manager

Already returning, Mme Giclefort?

Mme Giclefort

Don't speak to me about it. Mr. Giclefort makes me despair. He's a real greenhorn. Can you imagine that he let his belt out—pretending it was hot? (to Saint Franquet) Yes, sir. Then, naturally, he was taken by these little cramps.

Manager

Oh!

Mme Giclefort (to Saint Franquet)

He has very delicate intestines. It's his weak side.

Saint Franquet

Oh, truly, oh!

Mme Giclefort

Excuse me, but I prefer to go up, because when I am not there, he makes everything a mess.

Saint Franquet

Oh.

Mme Giclefort (curtseying)

Excuse me. (she leaves)

Saint Franquet

That woman is communicative, too.

Manager

Yes, but in fact, since you are a Parisian, you must have heard of her— It's the famous Stolzini.

Saint Franquet

The famous dancer—

Manager

Ah, yes sir, what a nice household—if monsieur knew—

Saint Franquet

Ah—her husband?

Manager

No—he's her lover.

Saint Franquet

Oh—

Manager

He's Mr. Giclefort, the proprietor of the "Pretty Gardener."

Saint Franquet

Ah—

Manager

Would you like to see your rooms?

Saint Franquet

Yes—yes—I've been told you have fine ones.

Manager

Thank you.

Saint Franquet

By Mr. Plantaredi and his wife.

Manager

But, they are here.

Saint Franquet

Are they? That's curious.

Manager

Would you like a room next to theirs?

Saint Franquet

That would be nice.

Manager

I won't give you the one next to Mme Plantaredi.

Saint Franquet

Why not?

Manager

Because it is much smaller.

Saint Franquet

I have a horror of large rooms.— Besides, it must be cheaper.

Manager

No—same price.

Saint Franquet

I'll take the one I prefer for the same price.

Manager

Then, I'll put you in number 13.

Saint Franquet

Fine! Fine.

(The Manager goes into the hotel. Plantaredi comes from the tennis courts with a racket.)

Plantaredi

Ah—Saint Franquet.

Saint Franquet (pretending astonishment)

For goodness sakes. If I had expected—

Plantaredi

What do you mean, if you had expected? You knew very well we were going to be here.

Saint Franquet

Me? Not at all!

Plantaredi

What do you mean, not at all? I myself told you, when you asked me where we were spending the summer.

Saint Franquet

I don't remember asking you—

Plantaredi

Come on, admit you came to find us—

Saint Franquet

Nothing of the sort!

Plantaredi

It would be nice.

Saint Franquet

I only came to get away—

Plantaredi

From what?

Saint Franquet

My nerves—I twitch at night, like I just got an electric shock.

Plantaredi

Then, you must leave immediately.

Saint Franquet

Why?

Plantaredi

The waters here are phosphorescent, radioactive, super-exciting.

Saint Franquet

Bah! I'll stay out of the waters.

Plantaredi

Why tell me these stories? You are here for us.

Saint Franquet (with energy)

No.

Plantaredi

Yes! Only, you don't want to say it, because you are afraid my wife might greet you coldly.

Saint Franquet

Me?

Plantaredi

I don't know why my wife has it in for you, my friend. But, she can't stand having you around.

Saint Franquet

Really?

Plantaredi

What do you want? Still, my friend, you are clumsy. One would say you didn't know women. To penetrate a household and show a preference for the husband alienates the wife.— It's well known, each time you visit, you say, "I come to see your husband." That's nice for my wife.

Saint Franquet

I hadn't looked at it that way.

Plantaredi

Wait! Here she is, right now, you are going to see. You are going to see her mind—

(Micheline comes in from the right, followed by Des Saugettes loaded down with umbrellas, rackets, mantles, etc.)

Micheline

Do you have everything, Des Saugettes?

Des Saugettes

I believe, yes, I have everything.

Micheline

Well—the camera.

Des Saugettes

Oh, my God! The camera. I left the camera.

Micheline

You have only to bring that, and you forget the camera.

Des Saugettes

I am unforgivable. I don't know how I could— Oh—

Plantaredi

Go, go—now, fetch it.

Des Saugettes

Yes, yes. (he runs out)

Plantaredi

Scatterbrain! Go!

Saint Franquet

Dear Madame.

Micheline

Mr. Saint Franquet, here!

Saint Franquet

Yes! Yes, Madame.

Micheline (icily)

Oh— Enchanted.

Plantaredi (to Saint Franquet)

Well—well— What did I tell you?— Her mind, eh?

Saint Franquet

But—no—I don't see.

Micheline (to Plantaredi)

What, "her mind, eh?" What do you mean by that— "Her mind, eh?"

Plantaredi

Nothing, nothing. I told him that when you should see him, you would show him your mind.

Micheline

Me?

Plantaredi

Yes, of course. And there it is. You can't stand the smell of him. That's a clear fact. And now he knows.

Micheline (shrugging her shoulders)

I can't stand the smell of him! Oh, that's stupid, what you are saying. I neither smell, nor not smell, Mr. Saint Franquet.

Saint Franquet

But evidently!

Des Saugettes (running in out of breath)

Here—here's—the camera.

Plantaredi

About time! You are winded?

Des Saugettes

No—oh, but give me your chair, you are burdened.

Saint Franquet

This isn't a man— It's a cloak room.

Plantaredi

Thanks. (letting Des Saugettes take everything) (to Saint Franquet) Now—I am going to present a charming boy to you— Mr. Des Saugettes.

Des Saugettes (touched)

Oh, Monsieur Plantaredi.

Saint Franquet

But, I've already had the pleasure of meeting him, just now.

Des Saugettes

Yes—sort of—

Saint Franquet

Running after a silk scarf, like a butterfly after a snare.

Plantaredi

Ah yes, my wife's scarf. But, that's not all. We've got to go in and change clothes. My wife and I are sweating.

Micheline

What? Speak for yourself.

Plantaredi

Well—so be it. I am sweating and my wife is perspiring.

Micheline

Not at all. What an idea!

Plantaredi

What— There's nothing to be ashamed of— My little Saugettes.

Des Saugettes

Sir.

Plantaredi

You are going to come up with me and give me a rub down.

Des Saugettes

But, with pleasure, sir.

Plantaredi (to Saint Franquet)

You have no idea how agreeable this boy is! He gives me a rub down every day.

Saint Franquet

Really?

Des Saugettes (flattered)

Oh, sir.

Plantaredi

And, he does a good job.

Des Saugettes

Oh, sir, truly!

Plantaredi

Yes, yes, no false modesty. Too bad he's well off. He'd make an admirable masseur.

Des Saugettes (laughing modestly)

Oh, you flatter me, Mr. Plantaredi, you flatter me.

Plantaredi

I speak as I think. (to Saint Franquet) If you have aches, pains, rheumatism, I recommend him to you.

Des Saugettes (very touched)

Oh, I am confused, really, I am confused.

Plantaredi

Give him a little massage.

Des Saugettes

With pleasure.

Saint Franquet

Very nice of you—but I don't have any rheumatism.

Des Saugettes

Oh—I regret—

Saint Franquet

Not me—but I'm touched all the same.

Plantaredi

Let's go. (to Micheline) And you, since you are not perspiring, well, are you going to keep company with your friend Saint Franquet?

Micheline

Me? Me?— But—

Plantaredi

But yes, but yes. (to Saint Franquet) Well, do you believe me now when I tell you she can't stand the smell of you? Do you believe it?

Micheline

Oh, please shut up—you are ridiculous.

Plantaredi

Oh—you'll have a hard time being sociable.

Micheline (between her teeth)

Imbecile!

Plantaredi

Yes, dear. (to Des Saugettes) Come, come, my appointed master. (he pushes him into the hotel in front of him) Till later.

Saint Franquet (with feeling)

Oh thanks, thanks, for those words of love which your husband just now uttered.

Micheline (dazed)

Huh! What? What words of love?

Saint Franquet

"You can't stand the smell of me."

Micheline

You find love in that?

Saint Franquet

Absolutely! For have I done anything to you? No— Then, why do you detest me, unless you're afraid you will fall in love with me?

Micheline

Oh, for heaven's sake. Talk about fatuousness.

Saint Franquet

Fatuous, perhaps—but it is based on observation.

Micheline

First of all, sir—what did you come here for?

Saint Franquet

Why, the waters—for depression.

Micheline

Come on, come on, tell that to someone else. You decided it was not enough to invade my domicile all winter, and to insinuate yourself into the good graces of my husband, having profited to the extent of implanting yourself in my house—in my household.

Saint Franquet

Oh— Oh.

Micheline

Let me speak! To the point where people began to gossip.

Saint Franquet

Why did these people mix in?

Micheline

—In what's none of their business! What? They have the right, indeed. And now, you have the cheek to come here to chase me again, to expose me—again—

Saint Franquet

But, not at all! I am a friend of your husband. I came to find him, that's very natural.

Micheline

There! There! What I just told you. Those are your tactics! (seeing the Gicleforts leave the hotel) And now, I beg you—in front of people— It wouldn't be past you to cause me a scene in public.

Saint Franquet

What?

Micheline

Smile—come on, smile!

Saint Franquet (dazed)

Yes—yes!

(Both force smiles on their faces.)

Mme Giclefort (to Mr. Giclefort)

Hurry! Come on, hurry! (They both sit on the bench and smile at Saint Franquet and Micheline) Well—it's over. The impudent little fellow has put on his belt.

Micheline and Saint Franquet

Oh!— Oh?

Mme Giclefort

Sir— Madame— (she and her husband leave)

Micheline (returning to the war)

It really is your tactic. For many years you knew my husband, and met him in your circle of acquaintances— And from when dates this colossal tenderness—huh?

Saint Franquet

From when?

Micheline (rising)

Don't lie! The date—I can be precise—was the date of the day after you first saw me with him.

Saint Franquet

Oh— And then? When would it be? When love dictated to me what you call "this tactic."

Micheline

Finally! You admit it.

Saint Franquet (rising also)

Yes, I admit it. I admit it, now that what I wanted to happen has happened. Your husband couldn't leave me alone until he introduced me to you. And then, that was the completion of my wishes. I was happy I could see you, live your life, breathe your air—you were there.

Micheline

You hear him! You hear him!

Saint Franquet

Why are you so sulky with me? Because I commit the crime of looking for a way to be near you?— But, have I once asked anything of you?

Micheline

No—but that will come.

Saint Franquet

Since I want to be your lover—

Micheline

You admit it, you admit it.

Saint Franquet

If one day, in a moment of weakness—you feel yourself disposed—to me—

Micheline

And, if in a moment of weakness, I felt myself disposed to you—?

Saint Franquet

In moments like that, if it's not me, it's someone else— Let it be me.

Micheline

So, so, it's out in the open. Well no, my friend, no—get it out of your head—I'll never be your mistress.

Saint Franquet

I don't know why you say things like that to me.

Micheline (pronouncing each word)

I…will…not…do…it!

Saint Franquet

Well—that's good. That's fine. (Micheline sits on the bench, a little time goes by) How badly you know me.

Micheline

Yes—pretty deception! It's for my husband's pretty eyes that you surround him with your kindness. And his charms made you want him to sit for his portrait.

Saint Franquet

You have no right to speak of that. You played that trick on me.

Micheline

You said you wanted to paint those features "which were most dear to you." I naturally thought you meant his.

Saint Franquet

That was a crude little trick of yours. But he was still a little part of you—so I made him as pretty as I could.

Micheline

He was very happy with it.

Saint Franquet

By God, he's never looked so good! Ah, why must I love you? (forcefully) Oh yes, I love you!

Micheline

Not so loud! Not so loud!

Saint Franquet (choking)

Oh yes, I love you.

Micheline

But, what's wrong with you? I've never seen you in such a state.

Saint Franquet

It's the water. It's the water. I haven't yet drunk any, but never mind, I feel regenerated already. It's the radioactivity. (rushing to her) Ah, Micheline! Micheline!

Micheline

You leave me alone! You leave me alone!

Saint Franquet

No, no, Micheline.

Micheline (pushing him, her flower falls off)

Pay attention— You broke my flower.

Saint Franquet

What does it matter? Micheline!

Micheline

Everything! People are coming.

Saint Franquet (picking up the flower)

Oh.

Micheline

Smile! Smile! (she sits down)

Saint Franquet (sitting, too)

Yes, yes. (smiles all around)

Manager (melon in hand)

Then—off the right—and you will find the spring on the left.

Tourists/Guests

Thanks. Thanks a lot.

(The Tourists, a bit astonished at the smiles of Micheline and Saint Franquet, return the grimaces and leave.)

Manager

Ah—you have found Madame Plantaredi.

Saint Franquet (irritated)

Yes! Yes.

Micheline (choking)

What? (she gets up sharply, as does Saint Franquet)

Manager (confidentially)

I am going to get a new melon, this one is too ripe.

Saint Franquet

Oh—oh—good.

Manager (bowing)

Monsieur, Madame. (he goes out)

Micheline

Oh really, you are mad! Have you been confiding in this man?

Saint Franquet

Oh, me, not at all! He told me you were here, and all I said was, "I'd be glad to see them."

Micheline

Now, who's going to believe that? Of the three hundred guests in the hotel, he just up and said the Plantaredis are here—and he doesn't know you from Adam.

Saint Franquet

It didn't happen that way at all.

Micheline (accompanying her words with nervous little taps on the table in front of her)

Oh—no, of course it didn't happen that way! Did you plan to do everything you could to compromise me?

Saint Franquet

Me? No!

Micheline

Yes, you.

Saint Franquet

She's worried.

Waiter (coming out of the hotel)

Did you want something, sir?

Saint Franquet (absently)

Worried. No, I didn't call you—it was the lady.

Waiter

What'll it be, mam?

Micheline

I want—I would like—

Saint Franquet

A piña colada—virgin.

Waiter

Yes, sir.

Micheline

What's a virgin?

Saint Franquet

No alcohol in it.

Micheline

What's that waiter going to think of me? You are completely crazy.

Saint Franquet

It doesn't matter to me what he thinks.

Micheline

But not to me! What am I? A woman who picks her nose? You have a way of mixing in everything—

Saint Franquet

Oh—no, no. (passionately) Oh, if you knew.

Micheline

Oh—no, no—you're not going to start all over again, are you? Anyway, give me my flower.

Saint Franquet

Your flower?

Micheline

Yes, my carnation.

Saint Franquet

You're not going to take it away from me? Are you?

Micheline

You are going to make me mad. (she tears the carnation from him)

Saint Franquet

Oh—you are cruel!

Micheline

Goodbye, dear sir.

Saint Franquet

I love you, Micheline.

Micheline

I forbid you to all me Micheline.

Saint Franquet

I love you, dear lady.

Micheline

Dear lady— Oh—you make me laugh.

Saint Franquet

That's it. Laugh! Laugh! When one laughs, one is half disarmed.

Micheline

But, you refuse to understand, my poor friend—I don't cheat on my husband.

Saint Franquet

That's very funny.

Micheline

Not at all!

Saint Franquet

Well—all the same, if you change your mind, by chance— Let it be with me!

Micheline (laughing)

No, really, you are laughable.

Saint Franquet

But damn it, you cannot love him.

Micheline

Who?

Saint Franquet

Your husband! Look at him. There he is in the window. He looks radiant. Radiant! Yes, bonjour, bonjour— Have a nice rub down. Go on!

Micheline

Don't you mock him. I won't stand for it.

Saint Franquet

I am not mocking him. But, look at him—with that imbecile— How can you love him? Has he got the figure of a lover?

Micheline

I thought it was you who loved him?

Saint Franquet

Certainly I love him. I love him like a friend—but not like a lover.

Micheline

Oh no, no—and that's enough. (Plantaredi disappears from the window) I warn you, if you start again, I'll call my husband.

Saint Franquet

If you think I'll give in to such threats— Call your husband. I still love you. There will be a brouhaha. At least, we'll have a situation.

Micheline

Oh—you defy me. Very well, it's you who asked for it. Antoine, Antoine.

Saint Franquet (seizing her hand and pulling her to him)

Oh no, no—you are not going to do that.

Plantaredi (opening the window)

Did you call me, my dear?

Saint Franquet

No, no!

Plantaredi

Hey, that's nice. Hand in hand. You are doing it for me. Bravo!

Saint Franquet

Eh, yes, yes, yes. (to Micheline) Right?

Micheline

Right.

Saint Franquet

Madame Plantaredi loves me now.

Micheline

What?

Saint Franquet

No—I mean—from now on, hostilities have ceased.

Plantaredi

L'Entente Cordiale! Bravo. Hey, have you seen my shorts, I can't find them?

Micheline

Wait, I'm coming up. (to Saint Franquet) With your permission.

Saint Franquet

I beg you.

Plantaredi

Was it difficult?

Saint Franquet

Oh!

Plantaredi

Don't repel her. It's all in knowing how to handle her.

Saint Franquet

Right.

Plantaredi

Excuse me. (he disappears inside)

Waiter (coming in with drinks)

The piña colada—virgin.

(Saint Franquet pays the Waiter. Dotty arrives, followed by Tommy.)

Dotty

Hurry up, Tommy. You're slow as a tortoise.

Tommy

It's because you walk so fast, Dotty.

Dotty (sees Saint Franquet and almost faints)

Oh— Shut up, Tommy!— Oh!

Tommy

What is it?

Dotty

Oh!

Saint Franquet (embarrassed)

Something must be wrong with me.

Dotty (going to him)

Bonjour, Monsieur.

Saint Franquet

Huh! Bonjour, Madame.

Dotty

No— Mademoiselle. Not married.

Saint Franquet (correcting)

Mademoiselle. Very pleased to meet you. (she shakes his hand and won't let go) But, you must be making a mistake, Miss. I can't recall ever meeting you before.

Dotty

Me either! I don't know you.

Saint Franquet (stunned)

Oh! Oh!

Dotty (presenting Tommy)

My fiancé.

Saint Franquet

Delighted.

Tommy (like a martyr)

Yes.

Dotty (to Tommy, while devouring Saint Franquet with her eyes)

Oh! How lovely. Isn't he, Tommy?

Tommy (scandalized)

What do you mean, Dotty?

Dotty

Oh, shut up, Tommy! Oh, lovely! Lovely!

Saint Franquet (dazed)

I beg your pardon, but—I just go there and—

Dotty

Oh, pardon, pardon.

Saint Franquet

Certainly—certainly—very happy.

Tommy (champing at the bit)

Oh! Oh! Oh!

Dotty (to Saint Franquet)

Are you staying for a while?

Saint Franquet

For a while—yes, yes.

Dotty

Oh—then, we'll go for walks together—you'll like that?

Saint Franquet

Huh? Oh! Certainly! Certainly Miss, Sir. (aside) It's got to be the waters here— Oh. (he escapes to the hotel)

Dotty

Oh, Tommy! Tommy! The young man is living in the hotel with us.

Tommy

Yes—but who is he?

Dotty

I don't know. I don't know him. I love him. I love him.

Tommy

But, Dotty, I am your fiancé.

Dotty

Yes. But, you promised you would do everything I wanted.

Tommy

That's true, but—

Dotty

Well—go tell him! I love him and I want to marry him.

Tommy

You're asking me to—? What about me?

Dotty

You can marry someone else. I am going to marry him.

Tommy

Dotty! I love you.

Dotty

Poor Tommy. And I love him. Oh, what wretches we are!

Tommy

I'm going to go have my head examined.

Dotty

Why, Tommy?

Tommy

'Cause I'm going to kill myself.

Dotty

But, Tommy, I love you very much. Only not for marriage. So, tell him I love him. I love him.

Tommy

Oh, oh! Never. Never. Better I kill him.

Dotty

Tommy, if you do that I will never marry you.

Tommy

And, if I don't do it?

Dotty

Then, I'll marry him.

Tommy (sitting down, head in hand)

Poor, poor Tommy.

Dotty (consoling him)

Don't cry, Tommy. Don't cry.

(Bichon appears with two partners who go off.)

Bichon

That's that. See you soon for revenge.

Dotty (pointing to Bichon)

Oh look, look. The little lady who ate near us in the restaurant.

Tommy

Yes.

Dotty

Oh, Miss—

Bichon

Me? Miss?

Dotty

Pardon—I wanted to ask you—I don't know how to say it—

Bichon

Go on, Miss. Go on.

Dotty

Are you a hooker?

Bichon (dazed)

What?

Dotty (in spite of signs from Tommy)

No, I mean—you are very—

Bichon (guardedly)

Yes, yes—I understand, I understand, Miss. Oh, but allow me—

Dotty

You're not angry?

Bichon

No! No!

Dotty

Then, you are a woman—for love?

Bichon (philosophically)

You might say that.

Dotty

And, all the men love you?

Bichon

There are not too many to complain of.

Dotty

Oh, tell me! Tell me! How do you do it?

Bichon

But, you are asking me to give you an education.

Dotty

Oh, tell me! Tell me! Yes, because I don't know. And I want to know how to make all the men love me.

Bichon

Oh! Oh?

Dotty

Because I love one fellow so much.

Bichon (interested)

Really? Who's that?

Dotty

I don't know. I don't know him. It's a thunderbolt.

Bichon (to Tommy)

Oh, isn't she sweet?

Dotty

Yes—a thunderbolt.

Tommy (sadly)

Dotty!

Dotty

Let me alone, Tommy! (to Bichon) This is my fiancé.

Bichon

Oh! Oh! (Tommy rises) My congratulations, sir.

Tommy (miserable)

Thanks.

Dotty

Because my father raises more hogs than anyone in America.

Bichon

Oh! Oh!

Dotty

He's a millionaire.

Bichon

To make millions with pigs!

Dotty

So, what shall I do?

Bichon

Well—if you love him—you must tell him.

Dotty

I asked my fiancé and (indignantly) he wouldn't do it for me!

Tommy (furious)

Oh no!

(Saint Franquet enters. Dotty sees him.)

Dotty

Oh, dear me, here he is.

Bichon (laughing)

No! Hey, Gerard!

Saint Franquet (annoyed)

Oh, Bichon again. (aloud) What?

Dotty

Oh, no. Be quiet!

Bichon (to Saint Franquet)

Can you imagine, this lady—?

Dotty

Oh no, no, I'm going. Come, Tommy—

Tommy

Yes—I'm coming. I hate that guy—

(Dotty and Tommy leave.)

Bichon

Well, old friend, can you imagine? You have inspired a passion.

Saint Franquet

Me?

Bichon

Yes. The little lady. The thunderbolt! Daughter of a millionaire. Wow, I adore you! This turns me on! (she hangs on his neck)

Saint Franquet (pushing her off)

Come, if someone saw you.

Bichon

Well— They would say you were getting on well.

Saint Franquet

Look—I'm very pleased to have found you again, but I'm here with some people—people of the world.

Bichon

What, then? Am I not a woman of the world?

Saint Franquet

That's not what I mean. (seeing Plantaredi) Oh, hell! (to Bichon) Go away! Go away. One of the people in question.

Bichon

Oh, that one—oh, my old friend.

Saint Franquet

What do you mean, "oh, my old friend"?

Bichon

Fine, perfect. (going) I haven't see you. I haven't seen you.

Saint Franquet (between his teeth)

What a tart!

Plantaredi (coming in)

Do you know that little woman there?

Saint Franquet

Me? Not at all. She was asking some information of me. The way to the spring.

Plantaredi

What nonsense—the spring. She goes there twice a day. She wanted to take a walk with you.

Saint Franquet

What do you want me to say? I don't know her.

Plantaredi

What a shame.

Saint Franquet

Why?

Plantaredi (checking to make sure his wife cannot hear him)

She pleases me a lot.

Saint Franquet

You are a serious man.

Plantaredi

Well, yes—serious. Serious in Paris— But here— Well, I feel a little raunchy.

Saint Franquet

And your wife?

Plantaredi

She? Oh, she intimidates me.

Saint Franquet (enchanted)

Truly?

Plantaredi

Honest women leave me cold.

Saint Franquet

Get out!

Plantaredi

I don't know how to say it. She's like the institution of marriage itself. It castrates me. One can say these things to a friend— She doesn't like it very much.

Saint Franquet (delighted)

With you?

Plantaredi

Certainly with me. And not with anyone else, for sure.

Saint Franquet

Yes— That's what I meant to say—

Plantaredi

The truth is, we are not well suited temperamentally.

Saint Franquet

Yes, yes—

Plantaredi

I am so passionate and she's frigid. Well, I think I've come to a turning point.

Saint Franquet

Yes—the coming of old age.

Plantaredi

Bah! I'm going to the spring.

Saint Franquet

To find the little woman?

Plantaredi

To drink my water. I'll be right back. If my wife comes, tell her.

Saint Franquet

Understood.

(Plantaredi leaves by the right. Bichon appears at the tennis nets.)

Bichon

Hep!

Saint Franquet

Huh! It's you again.

Bichon

Tell me—was it for this marriage you are making all that fuss?

Saint Franquet

What?

Bichon

Oh right, you know—do we have to repeat—because the wife—Aha. (she wiggles)

Saint Franquet

What do you mean—the wife, aha? What do you mean?

Bichon

She's like the others, my dear, like the others.

Saint Franquet (furious)

Like the others! I forbid you to say that.

Des Saugettes (leaving)

I ask your pardon. I am going to get Mr. Plantaredi's letters at the post office.

Saint Franquet

Yes, go— That's fine. (to Bichon) What do you mean—"the wife, aha?"

Bichon

Well, you have only to ask your friend.

Saint Franquet

What friend?

Bichon

The little gigolo—who's going to fetch the husband's letters. Oh, oh, my poor little old friend.

Saint Franquet

What are you insinuating?

Bichon

Nothing, nothing. I was wrong to tell you. I see you are vexed.

Saint Franquet

Me? I was going to kiss you.

Bichon

Really? Just try it.

Saint Franquet

Just so! (embracing her with rage)

Bichon

Watch out—someone's coming.

Saint Franquet

Oh—someone's looking. Still, I'll kiss you, tousle you. (seeing Micheline in the hotel door) Oh— Do you want to escape? Do you want to get away?

Bichon

Oh—little one—it's not my fault. (she wiggles out to the right)

Saint Franquet

What a tart that woman is!

Micheline

Oh, my congratulations and my excuses for coming so inopportunely to upset your amorous effusions.

Saint Franquet

It wasn't so bad.

Micheline (despite herself, a bit nervously)

A relative, no doubt.

Saint Franquet

Not at all. A coquette.

Micheline

At least you are frank.

Saint Franquet

Men are.

Micheline

What do you mean by that?

Saint Franquet

Men are frank, and women are not. They flaunt their virtue when they don't like the man who is prattling of love to them, but they know better than to talk that way to a gigolo who they prefer to flirt with.

Micheline

Your remark is directed at me?

Saint Franquet

I didn't name anyone. You recognize yourself rather quickly.

Micheline

If it wasn't directed at me, your remark wouldn't make any sense, therefore it is useless to play the Jesuit.

Saint Franquet

Then, you admit this little imbecile of a Des Saugettes—

Micheline

I admit nothing. Think what you like. I don't have to give an account to you—

Saint Franquet (pacing up and down)

True. Very true! (stopping) I am not sorry to have figured you out!

Micheline (also angry)

Good, good. (seeing Des Saugettes) Des Saugettes.

Saint Franquet (between his teeth)

The little puppet.

Des Saugettes

Here I am back.

Micheline (uneasily)

Yes, yes.

Saint Franquet (looking at Des Saugettes' buttonhole)

My word—he does have her flower.

Des Saugettes

Did you hear thunder? I believe we're in for it.

Saint Franquet

Yes—I think we're in for it, too.

Micheline

We'd better go in.

Des Saugettes

Willingly.

Saint Franquet

Ah—Mr. Des Saugettes—pardon me.

Des Saugettes

Dear sir?

Saint Franquet

What is that flower you are wearing?

Des Saugettes

It's a carnation.

Saint Franquet (breathing hard imitating Des Saugettes)

It's a carnation. You are an idiot.

Des Saugettes

Huh?

Micheline (afraid of a scandal)

Mr. Saint Franquet.

Saint Franquet

A carnation. I know enough about botany to recognize that.

Des Saugettes

But you asked me?

Saint Franquet

Yes. Well, sir, would you kindly withdraw this flower?

Des Saugettes

Huh?

Saint Franquet (drawing out his words)

Would you kindly withdraw this flower?

Des Saugettes

But—

Saint Franquet

Do you wish, sir, to withdraw this flower?

Micheline

I beg you, Mr. Saint Franquet.

Saint Franquet

And I beg you, too, Madame. This is a matter between the gentleman and myself.

Des Saugettes

Pardon, sir, I don't understand.

Saint Franquet

You haven't understood! It displeases me to see that flower in your buttonhole. Take it out.

(Lightning flashes.)

Des Saugettes

Sir, I'm not accustomed to—

Micheline (to Saint Franquet)

But, you have gone mad.

Saint Franquet

Exactly. I've gone mad.

(Thunder.)

Saint Franquet (to Des Saugettes)

If, in two seconds, you have not removed that flower, I will pull your ears off.

Des Saugettes (moving back a little)

Ah, but, sir—

Micheline

Mr. Saint Franquet!

Des Saugettes

Sir, you must know—

Saint Franquet (jumping)

Sir, sir. What are you saying, "I must know." "You dare me." "I must know." Do you hear that? I must know, I must know.

Micheline (overwhelmed)

Sir— Mr. de Saint Franquet.

Saint Franquet

Do you intend to remove that flower?

Des Saugettes

No, but listen—

Saint Franquet

You don't wish to withdraw it? As you please.

(Saint Franquet strikes Des Saugettes.)

Des Saugettes (holding his cheeks)

Oh—but look here. I am going to take it away.

Micheline (to Saint Franquet)

You are insane! You are losing your mind. By what right do you—?

Saint Franquet

Pardon me, Madame, I am the sole judge of my actions.

Micheline

This is too much!

(Lightning.)

Plantaredi (arriving)

How's the Entente Cordiale going?

(Thunder.)

Micheline

Oh, you are here. You came just in time. This gentleman—

Des Saugettes

Yes—can you imagine—

Saint Franquet

Let me explain.

Micheline

No sir, please. My husband wants me to speak.

Plantaredi

What? What? At it again?

Des Saugettes (pointing to Saint Franquet)

Can you imagine? I didn't say anything—

Plantaredi

Shut up, Des Saugettes.

Micheline

You are my husband. It's up to you to make them respect me.

Plantaredi

What—someone dared to show you lack of respect?

Micheline

You know my flower, my carnation—my carnation—well, Des Saugettes put it in his buttonhole.

Plantaredi (to Des Saugettes)

This is too much! Why? Why did you put this carnation in your buttonhole?

Des Saugettes

Me?

Micheline

But he's not at fault! Leave this child alone.

Plantaredi (to Des Saugettes)

Oh—sorry.

Des Saugettes

No problem.

Plantaredi

But, then who? Who?

Micheline (pointing to Saint Franquet)

This gentleman—who has just made an unspeakable scene and just struck Mr. Saugettes.

Saint Franquet

Right!

Des Saugettes

Yes—I don't understand, I said nothing to him.

Plantaredi

Can't you keep out of this! Leave us alone, okay?

Des Saugettes

Oh!

Micheline

Well—what do you think?

Plantaredi

Well—what do you mean? It was bothersome for Des Saugettes—

Micheline

Eh! Des Saugettes has nothing to do with this. It's a question of me! Of you!

Plantaredi

Of us?

Micheline

You find it natural for this gentleman to compromise me, making a scandal over this flower—

Saint Franquet

Excuse me! Excuse me!

Micheline

Yes, sir, you asked me, and it's because I refused you—

Saint Franquet

When can I speak—?

Des Saugettes

And then, apropos of nothing, without reason, I received a blow.

Plantaredi

Will you leave us in peace! No one is paying attention to you here.

Micheline

Oh, you admit that, you, you admit that?

Plantaredi

Not at all! (to Saint Franquet) My wife is right, sir. Can you explain to me?

Saint Franquet

Right, right, it's very good. If you think it is all right for this little gentleman to display in his buttonhole flowers people have seen your wife wear.

Micheline

That is not your concern!

Plantaredi

Absolutely!

Saint Franquet

If you allow this gigolo to make you ridiculous—

All Three

Ridiculous!

Plantaredi

"Ridiculous." Are you insinuating that my wife—?

Saint Franquet

No, but—

Plantaredi

Then, why are you mixing in?

Saint Franquet

Oh—if you take that tone—

Plantaredi

I take whatever tone pleases me.

Saint Franquet

Do you speak to me like that! Sir, you don't know me. You will have an affair with me.

Plantaredi

Useless to put on grand airs with me. Because I'm not a bully, do you believe you can frighten me?

Micheline

Well, you see him, your friend, you see him! And you reproach me for keeping him at a distance. You see, you can have confidence in him.

Des Saugettes

Oh no, I will remember this. To think how I put myself out to be nice to everyone— And because of a flower, I get hit in the face. Oh, not at all— This can go on forever.

Plantaredi

Enough. Let's stop this. (to Saint Franquet) Tomorrow, sir, you will receive my seconds.

Saint Franquet

Fine, sir, I am at your disposition.

Micheline (to Plantaredi)

My friend, my friend, you are not going to fight.

Manager (overwhelmed)

A fight. A fight in my hotel. Gentlemen, gentlemen, I beg you—

Plantaredi

Go take a walk.

Manager (submissively)

Yes. (to Saint Franquet) Sir, sir—for my hotel.

Saint Franquet

Go for your walk!

(The guests have come out to watch.)

Saint Franquet (to guests)

What do you want? Is this your affair?

Guests (disconcerted)

No—but—

Saint Franquet

Well, go eat! Go walk!

(The guests leave, grumbling.)

Micheline (to Saint Franquet)

Sir, your conduct is unworthy!

Plantaredi (to Micheline)

That's fine! That's fine. No more. (between his teeth) My God, how stupid this is.

Micheline (low to Des Saugettes)

As for you, why did you have to put that flower in your buttonhole?

Plantaredi

Yes. What did you do that for?

Des Saugettes

But, I didn't know, sir. It had fallen to the earth, and I didn't want to step on it.

Micheline

You are a little beast! A little beast!

Des Saugettes

I— Oh!

(They go into the hotel, leaving Des Saugettes behind.)

Saint Franquet (pacing in rage)

Oh! Oh! Oh!

Des Saugettes

Listen, sir, now we are alone—

Saint Franquet

Oh—you get to hell away from me or I'll break your face.

Des Saugettes (disconcerted)

Oh yes, sir, yes.

Saint Franquet

Tomorrow, my seconds.

Des Saugettes

As many as you like, sir, as many as you like. (going) Sacred name of God!

Bichon (rushing in)

What has happened? A dispute?

Saint Franquet

Oh—you—go to the devil!

Bichon

Huh!

Saint Franquet

Oh—rather, no. Come here, I adore you— (he pulls her to him)

Bichon

Huh?

Saint Franquet

Indeed, you are a real woman, you are honest. You make love, but you don't do it virtuously—you are honest.

Bichon

You are mad.

(Thunder.)

Saint Franquet

I love you, I adore you, I adore you. (embracing her with rage)

Bichon

Come on, come on, this is stupid, you are tickling me. Come on.

(Lightning.)

Saint Franquet

Never mind. You are honest. (repeated kisses)

(Violent thunder.)

Bichon

Come on—come on— (raining) Oh, fudge—it's raining.

Saint Franquet

I adore you.

(Tommy runs in, followed by Dotty, who is struck dumb

watching Saint Franquet cover Bichon with kisses.)

Tommy

Oh, look at him! Look at him!

Dotty

Oh! (emotionally) How he knows how to love.

Micheline (at the window)

Ah—your friend—look at him, your friend.

Plantaredi (at window)

Oh!

Saint Franquet

I adore you. I adore you.

Bichon (rising, pulling him to the hotel)

Fine—but it's raining too much, you can tell me upstairs.

Saint Franquet

Yes, I adore you. Certainly, I adore you.

Dotty

Oh—how lovely, how lovely.

(Giclefort and Mme Giclefort run in holding their heads under Madame's skirt. Bichon returns.)

Bichon

Get a load of that. (indicating the Gicleforts) Paul and Virginia!

(Thunder. Lightning.)

CURTAIN

ACT II

Saint Franquet's studio.

Before the curtain rises, you can hear Bichon singing, accompanied on the piano. Bichon is singing, skirts pulled up.

Bichon

Aha! Aha! Moya bot, bot, bot, bot, bot, bot, bot.

Troumali, Troumala. Aya Koulami, Aya Koulami.

Ki, ki, ki, ki, ki, ki, ki, ki.

(traipsing to the right, then to the left)

Moya bot, bot, bot, bot, bot, bot, bot.

Troumali, Troumala. Kakali, Kakala.

Zig, zig, zig, zig, ZIG!

(to her accompanist)

There, that's it. A good tempo after the second "aha." Then, I do my little shiver and then speed up on "moya bot," okay?

Accompanist (unseen)

Uh— Aha!

Bichon

Okay! One more time, then we'll stop. (she comes in as if making her entry)

En amoure, En alvadou si cousi cosa— voyalminett. Aya bougi.

Saint Franquet (in shirtsleeves surging like a waterspout)

Oh no, you can't be boring us with your song!

Bichon (jumping)

Boring.

Saint Franquet

Yes, boring. It's time. Is it going to go on forever—this serenade?

Bichon

It's not a serenade. It's a chansonette.

Saint Franquet

It's idiotic, your song.

Bichon

I regret. Doubtless, my dear, you don't understand it.

Saint Franquet

You mean you do?

Bichon

In every respect. I wrote it.

Saint Franquet

Oh! Fine.

Bichon

It's an Apache song.

Saint Franquet

So, what does it mean, Aya koumali, ki, ki, ki?

Bichon

First of all, it's "koulami."

Saint Franquet

Kohlami, if you like, I don't know the language ki, ki, ki. Kabali, kabala.

Bichon (disdainfully)

Oh, evidently, it means nothing the way you say it. But, when you put a little meaning, a little art— (she does)

Aya koulami, ki, ki, ki, ki, ki, ki, Troumali, troumala—kakali, kakala— Like that— It changes everything.

Saint Franquet (ironically)

Oh, yes, it changes completely.

Bichon

That is precisely the role of artists, to make clear to the public things which are not.

Saint Franquet (to accompanist)

Still, don't you find this idiotic?

Des Saugettes (appearing from behind the piano)

Yes, yes. (he has a big grin in his face)

Bichon

I didn't ask your opinion.

Des Saugettes

It was Gerard who asked me.

Bichon

Naturally. It would have astonished me if you were not of his opinion. You've licked his feet ever since he had that duel with you.

Des Saugettes

Me?

Bichon

Evidently, you are frightened.

Des Saugettes (laughing)

Oh, oh—I am frightened—

Bichon

And then, you mess me up with my song. Since you find it malicious to discourage an artist in the act of creation—

Saint Franquet (imitating her)

"In the act of creation."

Bichon

First of all, why are you here, anyway? It's almost two. If you don't go to the rehearsal, when will it be finished? Why aren't you dressed?

Saint Franquet

Why— Because I find nothing to wear— With your customary order.

Bichon

You find nothing to wear?

Saint Franquet

Evidently. You've arranged things so there is no servant in the house.

Bichon

Is that my fault? Victor asked to leave and Marie left without asking.

Saint Franquet

Wonderful. Why did Marie leave without asking?

Bichon

Because it's her day off.

Saint Franquet

And why did Victor ask to leave?

Bichon

Because it wasn't his day off.

Saint Franquet

That's beautiful. Charming. No wonder I can find nothing.

Bichon

Oh, no, no, this eternal grump. What? What? What can't you find?

Saint Franquet

I can't find the clothes brush.

Bichon (shrugging her shoulders)

You can't find the clothes brush! You can't find the clothes brush! Wonderful. It's in the kettle.

Saint Franquet

What do you say?

Des Saugettes (laughing)

It's in the kettle.

Bichon

Well, yes. It fell from my hands into the kettle. I didn't take it out. It's probably still there.

Saint Franquet

Oh—no—

Bichon

If you had looked—

Saint Franquet

You expect me to look in the kettle for a clothes brush?

Bichon

Naturally. Since it is there.

Saint Franquet

I ask very little of you. To ruin my brush—

Bichon

You didn't want me to wet my arm to the elbow, just for a brush!

Saint Franquet

Disgusting!

Bichon

My God, you are complicated!

Saint Franquet

How am I going to brush with a soaked brush?

Bichon

Is that all? Take mine. And that's the end of that.

Saint Franquet

Where is yours?

Bichon

In my suitcase, where would you expect?

Saint Franquet

Would I know? Possibly in the foot bath.

Bichon

Oh—how witty. (to Des Saugettes) And, as for you, you'd better shut up instead of taking Gerard's side.

Des Saugettes

I was of his opinion.

Bichon

The more reason for you to agree with me.

Des Saugettes

Oh—good—no, listen, since this makes Gerard upset—

Bichon

Oh, Gerard, always Gerard! I don't give a damn what upsets Gerard. He won't do this concert if I don't. I have my professional conscience. Go, go, my boy—get to work.

Des Saugettes (with a sigh)

Again.

Bichon (starts her song again in a rage, grumbling, bowing to right and left as she enters)

It's true. Always Gerard. But, does Gerard know anything? And then, I've had enough, every time I—

(The piano is playing and she begins to sing.)

Bichon

En Amoure, En Alvadou Si cousi, cosa voyalminett.

Aya bougi, leval troutrou

Gigouli pompan, aval trompet

Moravi Podi.

Atali popos.

Trin de al bou, si lim vabem

Roga bouf tane, mureiemir dalem!

Aha! Aha!

(Prolonged shivers.) Ah—

Refrain

Moya bot, bot, bot, bot, bot, bot.

Troumali, troumala.

Aya koulami aya koulami ki, ki, ki, ki, ki, ki, ki, ki!

Mayabot, bot, bot, bot, bot, bot, troumali, troumala.

(Saint Franquet enters, dressed in a jacket, singing with her.)

Both

Kakali, kabala. Zig, zig, zig, zig, zig!

Bichon

Idiot!

Saint Franquet

Oh, I know your song.

Bichon (letting her skirt fall)

Oh—then, you know it. Well? What do you want now?

Saint Franquet

The brush.

Bichon

The brush?

Saint Franquet

It wasn't in your suitcase.

Bichon

Impossible!

Saint Franquet

Why impossible?

Bichon

Because I put it there myself.

Des Saugettes

Listen, shall I go look?

Bichon

Yes, go, my friend—go—because of him.

Saint Franquet

Oh—if you think you're more thorough than I am.

Des Saugettes

Oh, I don't say that.

Bichon

Go anyway! Go.

Des Saugettes

Okay. (he leaves)

Bichon

No, you know, you are incapable of living with an artist.

Saint Franquet (shrugging his shoulders)

Oh—an artist.

Bichon

Yes, an artist. You don't take me seriously. You correct everything I say! In any case, I'm as much an artist as you. If you find something petty, you do it.

Saint Franquet

Painting has nothing to do with being petty.

Bichon

Before, it wasn't so bad. You painted like everything else. Now, it's little squares on top of each other.

Saint Franquet

Naturally. I am a parallelpipysdiste.

Bichon

That's not painting.

Saint Franquet

It's a school.

Bichon

Well—so much the better. In any case, you paint as you like, and I don't criticize you. Well—do the same when I practice my art.

Saint Franquet

I preferred when you were a good girl, without pretensions, with your hair brown—which you have now bleached.

Bichon

Only blondes succeed in musicals.

Saint Franquet

When you called yourself "Bichon," not Blanche de Jouy. (contemptuously) Blanche de Jouy! What's this?

Bichon

What?

Saint Franquet (pulling the brush from the armchair)

Your brush.

Bichon

You found it?

Saint Franquet

Under the cushion!

Bichon

Well—you see—you have to look.

Saint Franquet

Oh—right.

Bichon

I told you I put it somewhere.

Saint Franquet (brushing his jacket)

Oh, yes. That's right. Ah, you're well organized.

Des Saugettes (returning)

Well, you know, I looked in the suitcase very carefully, and I could not find the brush.

Saint Franquet

Yes, you might have looked there a long time.

Des Saugettes

You found it?

Saint Franquet

Naturally. In the armchair.

Des Saugettes (laughing)

In the armchair. Oh!

Bichon

Indeed, in the armchair. (to Saint Franquet) Now—what do you need now?

Saint Franquet (looking on the table)

My ticket to the rehearsal. Where did you put it? It was on the table.

Bichon (bored and resigned)

In the bathroom—on the mantle-piece.

Saint Franquet

Wasn't there, I looked.

Bichon

It must have fallen. I put it there myself.

Saint Franquet

Go look.

Bichon

Oh—not even capable of— (shoving Des Saugettes) Oh—let me be. (she leaves)

Saint Franquet

Ah—this mess.

Des Saugettes

My poor friend, Women, eh?

Saint Franquet

Wonderful times, in the name of God.

Bichon (returning)

Well, I knew very well it was there.

Saint Franquet

You found the ticket?

Bichon

Naturally.

Saint Franquet

On the chimney?

Bichon

No—in it.

Saint Franquet

Oh—yes—I should have known.

Bichon

Yes—here!

Saint Franquet

What's this? Well, what is this?

Bichon

It's the ticket—I'm sorry, it's slightly damaged.

Saint Franquet

Yes—so I see.

Bichon (defensively)

It fell in the fireplace. It's still good.

Saint Franquet

You don't expect me to present this rubbish to the ticket office, do you?

Bichon

Why not? You don't have to explain to them what happened.

Saint Franquet

And, if they ask?

Bichon

Well, then, tell them I did it! Don't make such a big scene about everything! Here's your hat.

Saint Franquet

Well, put it there. I'll take it when I'm ready.

(Angrily, Bichon goes to put it on a chair and knocks over a painting on an easel by accident as she returns.)

Bichon

Oh—shit—oh!

Saint Franquet

What? What this time?

Bichon

It's your nasty picture. You left it there, like that—it's not dry—and naturally, when someone goes by—

(The picture is ruined.)

Saint Franquet (running to the picture)

My God! What have you done?

Bichon

Well, I had my hands full, and I didn't see it.

Saint Franquet

You have ruined my painting. Oh—this is nice. Name of God. This is agreeable.

Bichon

My new corsage!

Saint Franquet

But, I don't care about your corsage. It can croak, your corsage. My picture!

Bichon

I don't care about your picture! It can croak!

Saint Franquet

A painting which I just finished. Which I only had to sell.

Bichon

As for this mania of painting in oils—a substance which dries.

Saint Franquet

What do you expect me to paint in—vinegar?

Bichon

Oh, no! This is what it's like to have a painter for a lover.

Saint Franquet

Well, leave him—your painter—leave him. He won't keep you.

Des Saugettes

Children, children.

Saint Franquet

You—keep out of this!

Des Saugettes

Yes.

Bichon (throwing her corsage)

And go find me my—

Des Saugettes

Yes, I'll go look for it. (he leaves)

Bichon

If you think that I'll cling to you!

Saint Franquet

Well, then!

Bichon

Thank God, I wouldn't be tied down. And, I know more than one.

Saint Franquet

Well, take them—your more than one—take them.

Bichon

You don't have to say that to me twice.

Des Saugettes (returning)

Here it is.

Bichon

Thanks. (to Saint Franquet) You don't have to say it twice to me.

Saint Franquet

Fine

Des Saugettes

What's wrong?

Bichon (choked up)

I am going, Des Saugettes, I am going!

Des Saugettes

Children—please.

Bichon

No, no— Why continue a situation in which there is no love on either side?

Des Saugettes

Oh, there is, there is.

Bichon

There is not. Why waste words? He doesn't love me, I don't love him.

Des Saugettes

You do, you do.

Bichon

For a long time Gerard has spoken in eloquent silences— (shrugging her shoulders, then to Saint Franquet) Say it's not so!

Des Saugettes

It isn't. It isn't.

Bichon

I'm not asking you! One isn't in the habit of calling on you in such moments.

Saint Franquet

Oh, I beg you, tell him the details!

Bichon

Oh—no need. He can see us. He must stare! He ought to know that if we are together, it's not precisely from a great love. As for me, I was turned on because that little American girl went crazy about you.

Saint Franquet

Poor thing—

Bichon

You—from anger because your married woman sent you packing because she preferred to sleep with Des Saugettes.

Saint Franquet

What?

Des Saugettes

Huh? Excuse me! Oh.

Saint Franquet (to Bichon)

First of all—you lie! Never did Des Saugettes do what you said with her.

Des Saugettes (between them)

Absolutely never!

Bichon

Yes! (pushing Des Saugettes aside) Then, why did you wound him in a duel?

Saint Franquet (pushing Des Saugettes out of the way)

Because I didn't know it.

Bichon (again pushing Des Saugettes)

Oh—to enter into relations.

Des Saugettes

In any case—never, absolutely never!

Bichon

Yes, you did, yes, you did!

Saint Franquet (to Des Saugettes)

You don't need to defend yourself, I know the person in question. She's an honest woman.

Bichon (ironically)

Oh—yes.

Des Saugettes

But, absolutely!

Saint Franquet

And then, she's a woman of taste.

Des Saugettes

Absolutely. (then, correcting himself, offended) Oh, you say that you—

Saint Franquet (continuing)

Who doesn't give herself to the first imbecile who comes along.

Des Saugettes

Oh—what are you saying?

Saint Franquet

Oh—shut up! How could you attract an honest woman, the way you behave?

Des Saugettes

If the discussion is going to take this turn, I'd better go.

Saint Franquet

Well—go. Who asked you to stay?

Des Saugettes

When you've finished, you can call me.

Saint Franquet

And, besides, you have a bad character—

Des Saugettes (going)

You're right, yes, I am very stupid. Ah—I'm very stupid. (he leaves)

Saint Franquet

Ah—there, yes—have you seen—?

Bichon

Oh, it was a long while ago that I told you, when a friend insinuates himself into a household.

Saint Franquet

Ah—yes— Oh—but!

(Long silence.)

Bichon (taking a step toward him)

Gerard.

Saint Franquet

What?

Bichon

Give me your hand.

Saint Franquet

What's the use?

Bichon

Yes. We are saying useless hurtful things to each other. It's stupid! Go on! Give me your hand.

Saint Franquet

No.

Bichon

And let's separate!

Saint Franquet (giving her his hand with emotion)

Ah! Yes!

Bichon

Let's separate— But stylishly—like good friends! Like two beings who loved each other well, who esteem each other, but who cannot stand each other.

Saint Franquet

You're right. That's the best way.

Bichon (leaning against him)

And, besides, you know, I have no scruples. I have someone.

Saint Franquet (bowled over)

What?

Bichon

Yes, seat 49.

Saint Franquet

What do you mean, seat 49?

Bichon

A frequenter of my club. He didn't waste a minute. He sent me flowers and burning letters.

Saint Franquet

On my compliments. You've carefully kept this from me.

Bichon

A lover is like a husband; there are certain things you don't tell him.

Saint Franquet

Betray his confidence.

Bichon

Oh! But I've never betrayed yours. I'm sentimental. Why, the other day, chair 49 sent me this earring with a note that if I wanted the mate, he would bring it to me.

Saint Franquet

The impudent!

Bichon

Possibly. But, you must admit, it was tempting. Well, I didn't want him to. I sent word. There was no reply. As for the solitaire—

Saint Franquet

You sent it back.

Bichon (with dignity)

No. But I keep it in my purse. See what I did for you!

Saint Franquet

You're too good!

Bichon

That's the way I am.

Saint Franquet

Well—no more sacrifices for you. Go find chair 49. Go! Go!

Bichon

Oh—it's not difficult. One phone call and he'll be here.

Saint Franquet

Well, do it then. Don't put yourself out for me.

Bichon

No? Well, this won't take long. (she takes the receiver off the hook)

Saint Franquet

You're going to call him from here?

Bichon

I don't need to tell him where I am. Shut up. I'm listening. Is this chair 49? (simpering) It's Mlle de Jouy speaking.

Saint Franquet

What the hell.

Bichon

Yes. Don't trouble yourself. Come, right away. I'll be waiting at 27, Faubourg St. Honoré. (pause) You're coming—good! (she hangs up)

Saint Franquet

Ah, this is outrageous. You are mad. You're bringing him to my house!

Bichon

But he doesn't know it's your house.

Saint Franquet

That's all the same to me. You don't give a damn! I refuse to play a ridiculous role.

Bichon

Anyway, you can leave before he gets here.

Saint Franquet

It's agreed, we'll separate. But my replacement isn't going to make his scene on my furniture— Oh, no! (he grabs the receiver)

Bichon

What are you going to do?

Saint Franquet (waving paper)

Is this the number? (he dials)

Bichon (running to him)

Gerard! Gerard! Come on.

Saint Franquet

Let me alone!

Bichon

What you are doing is ridiculous, Gerard.

Saint Franquet

That's all right with me. Hello. (to Bichon) It's his wife?

Bichon

Gerard, will you stop?

Saint Franquet

Leave me alone! (into phone) No, I don't want to speak to you. Oh—you are his wife? Well, tell your husband he's a rake.

Bichon (scandalized)

Oh!

Saint Franquet

And, that the lover of Mlle de Jouy says to kiss his ass. (pause) What am I talking about? I'll tell you. Your husband is trying to make it with Mlle de Jouy. (pause) How do I know? She told me! Yes, and he's on his way here now.

Bichon

Oh, really, you've gone mad, haven't you?

Saint Franquet

My respects, ma'am. (pause) Where am I? At 27, Faubourg St. Honoré. (pause) Oh—yes, ma'am, we'll be waiting.

(Bichon tears the telephone from his hands.)

Bichon

You leave things alone!

Saint Franquet (furious, walking around her)

Ah, then, you, you are going to give me the pleasure of leaving, and then I won't have to put up with you anymore.

Bichon

You lift your hand to me? (calling) Des Saugettes! Des Saugettes. Help.

Saint Franquet

Have you finished screaming?

Des Saugettes (running in)

What's wrong?

Bichon

It's Gerard. Gerard's beating me.

Des Saugettes

Oh!

Saint Franquet (to Bichon)

I beat you? I beat you? No, little trouble-maker. (giving her little taps on the fat of her arm) Do I look like a wife beater? Do I?

Speak— Is that the way I act?

Bichon

Oh—calm down, calm down!

Des Saugettes

Come on, come on!

Saint Franquet

Can you imagine? Madame allows herself to telephone from here, to I don't know who—to chair 49, and gives him a rendezvous here, to accord him her favors. (tapping her) I beat you! I beat you?

Bichon (crying)

Des Saugettes! Des Saugettes!

Des Saugettes

Look—come on, that's enough!

Saint Franquet

Leave me alone, you! (someone rings the doorbell) And now, go answer that, since Madame has given the servants leave.

Des Saugettes (hesitating)

Yes—but don't beat her anymore.

Saint Franquet

I'm saving myself for chair 49. I'm going to give it to your chair 49.

Bichon

You will pay me for this, you know, you will pay me.

Saint Franquet

Yes. Fine. That's understood.

Bichon (folding her arms)

Go! Swine.

(Des Saugettes enters, with an enormous vase of flowers.)

Saint Franquet (to Des Saugettes)

What? What is this?

Des Saugettes

It's flowers.

Saint Franquet

Yes—from chair 49. Wait a bit, while I throw them out the window.

Des Saugettes

But, they're for you.

Saint Franquet

For me?

Bichon (bitterly)

There! Look at that! That's too much!

Saint Franquet

What can it mean—for me? Who sent them?

Des Saugettes

I don't know. They wouldn't say. But, it was for you.

Saint Franquet

No cards?

Des Saugettes

No cards.

Saint Franquet (pointing to console)

Put them there.

Des Saugettes

They are pretty flowers.

Bichon

Now that they are for you, you are not going to throw them out the window, right? Say something!

Des Saugettes

Come on, come on. (to Saint Franquet) If you are going to the rehearsal—

Saint Franquet

I am not going!

Bichon

Ah!

Saint Franquet

I am staying here. I'm waiting for him—chair 49.

Des Saugettes

Chair 49?

Saint Franquet

To kick his ass.

Bichon (with a smile of pity)

Imbecile!

Saint Franquet

Oh—go on, talk—you.

Bichon

Then, you think, really—he's going to come?

Saint Franquet

What?

Bichon

You think I'm naïve enough to telephone him in front of you. What, am I stupid?

Saint Franquet

Come on, come on. Tell someone else!

Bichon

If you had looked closely! I had my hand on the receiver, and I wasn't talking to anyone. To give you a lesson and enrage you.

Saint Franquet

Oh—you pretend to me now?

Bichon

The proof is, when you dialed the same number, you got a woman. A poor creature you completely upset with your stupid maneuver.

Saint Franquet

You're right. I'll call back—

Bichon (excited)

Ah—no!

Saint Franquet

You see—you're pulling my leg.

Bichon

Fine! Fine! I make up stories and tell you!

Saint Franquet

If you think you are going to make me believe—

Bichon

Fine—stay—you will see.

Saint Franquet

Women are capable of such cynicism!

Bichon

That's fine. Stay, I tell you. You will get it.

Saint Franquet

I'll stay if I want to! I suppose I have to miss my rehearsal to please you!

Bichon

Well, go.

Saint Franquet (gesticulating wildly while Bichon tries to get by him)

Well, I'm going! If you believe I swallowed your little story with the telephone— Oh, you thought to fool me, but I fooled you.

Bichon

Oh, fine.

Saint Franquet

You're not going to trick me. As for you, Des Saugettes, you have nothing to do, so stop by the florist, and find out who sent me those flowers.

Des Saugettes

Understood.

Bichon (to Saint Franquet)

Oh—that intrigue.

Saint Franquet

No, Madame, no. But I'd like to know. I don't want anyone to take me for a coquette. Goodbye! (he leaves, slamming the door)

Des Saugettes

These flowers are so pretty.

Bichon

There, he's gone. Well, now, my little Des Saugettes, you are going to please me by clearing out.

Des Saugettes

What?

Bichon

I'm waiting for someone, I don't need you.

Des Saugettes

You are waiting for someone?

Bichon

Yes.

Des Saugettes

Who? Who?

Bichon

I told you, someone—someone you don't know who's waiting for me, and not for you.

Des Saugettes

Oh, my God. Chair 49.

Bichon

How clever you are!

Des Saugettes (indignant)

Oh, oh! Bichon! It's not possible. You just said yourself it wasn't true. You only pretended to telephone.

Bichon

Poo!

Des Saugettes

Oh, why, why did you tell Gerard—?

Bichon

Why, so he'd go.

Des Saugettes

Bichon—I don't believe it, you wouldn't do that in front of him.

Bichon

I do everything in front of people. I don't like mysteries. And then, the nice part is, they don't believe it.

Des Saugettes

You are cynical.

(The doorbell rings.)

Bichon

Well, here he is.

Des Saugettes

Oh, no. I prefer to go.

Bichon

Notice, that's all I ask of you. I'll go open the door and you leave that way. Agreed?

Des Saugettes

Oh no, no—! And, this in front of me—to make me an accomplice. Oh!

(Des Saugettes goes out by the left. Prolonged ringing.)

Bichon

Come in, monsieur, come in.

Plantaredi (all dolled up)

Oh, I am so happy. My little Jouy, my little Jouy.

Bichon

Come, come, sir, I beg you—

Plantaredi

Oh, when I think this is the little woman that I applaud twice a week—and now, we are together—you and I.

Bichon

Yes.

Plantaredi

But, no boasting, my hand touches yours. Oh, when you telephoned me just now, I was so happy—my wife came. I got rid of her.

Bichon

Oh, you are married?

Plantaredi

I am married, yes—but, let's not bother ourselves about that. Oh—I rushed over here. I jumped in a cab. And, here I am. My little Jouy— my little Jouy.

Voice of Des Saugettes

Oh, it's disgusting, what you've done, sir. My friend's girlfriend.

Plantaredi (stunned)

What was that?

Bichon

Nothing! Nothing!

Voice of Des Saugettes

Go away, sir, go away!

Plantaredi

But, who is talking like that?

Bichon

It's— It's someone I was rehearsing with. He's repeating his lines. Wait. (opening the door at the left) Leave, my friend, leave! I told you I have no more need of you.

Voice of Des Saugettes

It's disgusting.

Bichon (kicking Des Saugettes)

Go! (Des Saugettes escapes) He's gone.

Plantaredi

It wasn't Dramen? It seems to me I recognized his voice.

Bichon

No, no—it was not Dramen.

Plantaredi

In any case, he's a good actor. Such conviction!

Bichon

Yes, he's a boy who will go far.

(At this moment, Des Saugettes' head appears over the short curtain, trying to see what is going on. Bichon sees him, and makes a threatening face. He disappears, and we hear the door close violently.)

Plantaredi

Ah—there, he's just gone.

Bichon

Yes.

Plantaredi (amorous)

We are finally alone!

Bichon

Yes, yes.

Plantaredi

Ah—how happy I am.

Bichon (looking him over seriously)

It's curious. Your face is familiar. Surely, I've seen you in the papers.

Plantaredi

Oh—not likely.

Bichon

Why?

Plantaredi

Because they never take my picture.

Bichon

Huh! That's funny. They put everybody in the papers these days. Still, I've got your face in mind. You must be famous.

Plantaredi

I wish. But, no.

Bichon

Then, your only name is chair 49?

Plantaredi

Oh, no.

Bichon

Well?

Plantaredi (after hesitating)

Antoine.

Bichon

That's nice. Then what?

Plantaredi

Isn't that enough for you today?

Bichon

Oh no, no, I love to know who I am talking to. Come on, your name?

Plantaredi (after a new hesitation)

Mr. Voltaire.

Bichon

Bah! Clearly you are someone well known.

Plantaredi

It's funny, for me too. I have the feeling this isn't the first time I've seen you.

Bichon

Oh—well, in any case, we've never been together before! Because I have a memory for such things.

Plantaredi

No, no. I don't pretend that! Wait! You don't have a sister who you resemble, and who is—not in the theatre?

Bichon

Not in the theatre? It might have been me, before I went on stage.

Plantaredi

You resemble a little woman called Bichon.

Bichon

Bichon? But, I am Bichon!

Plantaredi

Bichon! You are Bichon. That's why you look like her. Do you remember—Chatel-Sancy?

Bichon (nonplussed)

No—the gentleman whose wife—?

Plantaredi

Whose wife?

Bichon

Nothing! Oh, this is funny. And, you've made up—you know, you look like someone.

Plantaredi

My wife insists I wear my hair this way.

Bichon

You look like Gerard de Saint Franquet.

Plantaredi

You know him?

Bichon

He's my lover.

Plantaredi (rising)

What?

Bichon

This is his flat—studio.

Plantaredi

How do I get out of here?

Bichon

Don't move. He's at the rehearsal of the Comédie Française. You have plenty of time.

Plantaredi

But, that rehearsal— It's tomorrow.

Bichon

What? Are you sure?

Plantaredi

Absolutely. I am going. Faroudy is playing in Nantes. The rehearsal was delayed.

Bichon

Oh, for God's sake! Then Gerard—?

Plantaredi

Oh, indeed, Gerard.

(At this moment, one hears the vestibule door shut.)

Bichon

Shit. It's him.

Plantaredi

Oh, dear. Oh, dear.

Bichon (opening the door to the room on the left)

Quick, this way! At the back door, turn right, and the door to the right.

Plantaredi

Yes, yes, the door to the right. (he exits left)

Bichon (slightly troubled, to Saint Franquet)

What? It's you.

Saint Franquet (entering, crossly)

It's tomorrow.

(Saint Franquet takes his palettes and easels and starts rearranging them. This hides him from view. At this instant Plantaredi falls like a bomb into the studio.)

Bichon

Oh! (forgetting) Not that way! Not that way!

Plantaredi

Door to the right! Door to the right!

Bichon

No—to the left. To the left!

Saint Franquet (sorting his paints)

To the right? To the left? What?

Plantaredi and Bichon

Oh!

Saint Franquet (seeing Plantaredi, who tries to hide his face with his hat)

What do you want, sir?

Plantaredi

Here—I—I— You don't have a painting to sell?

Saint Franquet

Huh! But, it's Plantaredi.

Plantaredi (instinctively denying it)

No.

Saint Franquet

What do you mean, no?

Plantaredi

Yes!

Saint Franquet

Oh, no, it's not possible. Plantaredi here! It's Plantaredi. Oh, my dear friend! (giving him his hand) How are you doing?

Plantaredi

Not bad, thanks.

Bichon (to herself)

This is working out better than I thought.

Saint Franquet

It's really nice to see you again. It was too stupid, our quarrel. And, how's the wife?

Plantaredi

My—my wife? Yes, yes, she's fine.

Saint Franquet

I can't believe my eyes. Plantaredi—Bichon, this is Plantaredi. Plantaredi, of whom I have spoken so often. I have never introduced you— My good friend, Plantaredi, my dear friend, Mlle de Jouy.

(Plantaredi and Bichon bow, as if they had never met before. Then it dawns on Saint Franquet and he looks at both.)

Saint Franquet

I am a fool. Oh.

Bichon

What?

Saint Franquet

Chair 49.

Bichon

Ridiculous.

Plantaredi

What?

Saint Franquet (between his teeth)

Oh! You are chair 49.

Bichon (quickly to Plantaredi)

Your ass! Watch your ass!

Plantaredi (instinctively putting his hat over his behind)

Huh?

Bichon

Watch out! He said he would beat it.

Plantaredi

Huh?

Saint Franquet (calming down)

No—no— Don't be afraid. I said that when the ass was anonymous. But, now that I know to whom the ass has the honor to belong—it is sacred to me. The ass of an old friend like you.

Plantaredi (breathing again)

Oh! Fine.

Saint Franquet

But, I am happy at the coincidence that gives me the pleasure of meeting you again.

Plantaredi

A pleasure shared—indeed.

Saint Franquet (shaking hands)

Dear Plantaredi.

Plantaredi

Dear Saint Franquet.

Bichon (dazed)

I'm the one who is in shock.

Saint Franquet

So, you came here, my good Plantaredi, with the intention of cuckolding me?

Plantaredi

Yes! (withdrawing) No!

Saint Franquet

Don't defend yourself. It's all part of life. Today you, tomorrow me— Because there will always be men and women.

Plantaredi

Yes, but all the same, I had no idea you—didn't know you had a lover.

Saint Franquet

Well, I don't.

Bichon

No!

Saint Franquet

You can give her the other earring.

Bichon

I told him everything.

Saint Franquet

You've fallen in luck. The place is empty. I give her to you. Happy to do it.

Plantaredi

To me?

Bichon (vexed)

How dare you! "Happy to do it."

(Saint Franquet pushes Bichon toward Plantaredi.)

Bichon (pushing away)

I know how to give myself without any help from you.

Saint Franquet

Don't I know.

Bichon

To listen to you, one would think you were throwing me out.

Saint Franquet

No—not at all.

Bichon

I beg to tell you, sir, I am not a woman you can throw out. I do the throwing.

Saint Franquet (conciliating)

Right! Right!

Bichon (half enraged, half laughing)

You are irritating me; stop!

Plantaredi

No, Saint Franquet, you're joking.

Saint Franquet

Not at all. I'm serious.

Plantaredi

Gerard!

Saint Franquet

You're dying for her.

Plantaredi

No, no.

Bichon

Oh, indeed. Keep talking, sweetheart.

Plantaredi

That's not what I mean. What I mean is— (he stops)

Saint Franquet

You've got to say something.

Plantaredi

You are putting me in a situation. Are you sincere?

Saint Franquet

Yes.

Plantaredi

Well, then. So be it!

Bichon

Oh—no!

Plantaredi

I am so—touched. Bichon.

Bichon (taking him in her arms)

Poor thing.

Saint Franquet

Let anyone say I am jealous! (doorbell rings) Someone's ringing. Don't disturb yourselves. I'll get it. (he leaves)

Plantaredi

Then—we're together.

Bichon

It looks that way.

Plantaredi

I am very happy.

Bichon

Do you have the second earring?

Plantaredi

Yes.

Bichon

You want to give it to me, huh?

Plantaredi

You bet!

Saint Franquet (coming back)

Children.

Bichon

Eh!

Saint Franquet

I've got to get you out of here. Someone's coming.

Bichon

Who?

Saint Franquet

My sister.

Bichon

You don't have one.

Saint Franquet

That doesn't matter.

Bichon

Okay. We'll go in here.

(They go into a bedroom. After a moment, Dotty and Tommy come in.)

Saint Franquet

Mlle Dotty— Come in. Come in, please.

Dotty (followed by Tommy)

You are surprised! I took the chance. But, you recognized me— which was sweet.

Saint Franquet

Miss, when one has once had the pleasure—

Dotty

I've always thought of you. Haven't I, Tommy?

Tommy (bitterly)

Yes!

Dotty

This is my fiancé.

Saint Franquet

Yes, I know.

Dotty

You recognize him? Good! (going to bedroom door) What's this?

Saint Franquet

No, Miss Dotty. That's my bedroom.

Dotty

Well—may I?

Saint Franquet

No, no— Don't go in there, Miss. The room isn't made.

Dotty (going to the right)

And what's this?

Saint Franquet

Toilette.

Dotty

Is it made up?

Saint Franquet

Yes.

Dotty

Right. Tommy.

Tommy

Dotty.

Dotty

Go in there.

Tommy

Why?

Dotty

Because I say so.

Tommy

Oh.

Dotty

I have no need of you. Go, go— (pushes him out)

Tommy

All right, Dotty. (he leaves, piteously)

Dotty

Terrible, that man. He always asks why. Why? Because I say so! (changing tone) And now—for you— Did you receive my flowers?

Saint Franquet

What? That was you?

Dotty

It was.

Saint Franquet

Why?

Dotty

Mr. Gerard. Do you want to marry me?

(Saint Franquet is stunned. He doesn't make any reply.)

Dotty

You don't want to? Don't I please you?

Saint Franquet

Yes, you please me.

Dotty

Oh—thanks.

Saint Franquet

I'm very flattered. I would even say very touched. But—I'd have to think about it.

Dotty

Oh—I understand. Take all the time you want. (as if she was giving him forever) I give you five minutes.

(Dotty goes towards his pictures with an air of giving him time to think things over.)

Saint Franquet

But, you don't know me.

Dotty

We'll get to know each other. Is that your only objection?

Saint Franquet

You are very rich.

Dotty

Is that an objection?

Saint Franquet

Yes.

(There is a knocking on the toilette door.)

Tommy

You haven't forgotten me?

Dotty

No, wait, wait! Go away!

Tommy

Sorry!

(Tommy goes off.)

Saint Franquet

Yes—I will marry you.

Dotty

Then, everything is arranged!

Bichon (appearing at the door)

Hey, Gerard. Oh—excuse me! I forgot!

Dotty (not at all disconcerted)

Mademoiselle!

Bichon

Bonjour, Miss. Don't be disturbed. Don't be disturbed. (to Plantaredi who cannot be seen) It's his sister!

Dotty (to Saint Franquet)

That's Miss Bichon, right?

Saint Franquet

Huh? Err—yes!

Dotty

Your mistress?

Saint Franquet

My—Mis—? No—no.

Dotty

Oh, you can say it. Very nice. Very chic.

Saint Franquet (flattered)

You think so?

Dotty

Yes. I congratulate you. When we are married you must kick her out.

Saint Franquet

Oh! Oh!

Dotty

Yes—I prefer that.

Saint Franquet

Yes. I'll write to her.

Dotty

No hurry. This evening.

Saint Franquet

This evening. Yes.

Dotty (rising)

Goodbye.

Saint Franquet

Where are you going?

Dotty

Oh—we've said everything. I have errands to run. Do you love me?

Saint Franquet

Do—I love you!

Dotty

Well! I'm happy. Kiss me!

Saint Franquet

My dear fiancée. (they kiss)

Dotty

Oh—where is it?

Saint Franquet

You forgot something?

Dotty

Yes, my fiancé. Where did I put him?

Saint Franquet (pointing)

There.

Dotty (opening the door)

Come along, Tommy! It's over.

Tommy (coming back)

Not soon enough.

Dotty (to Saint Franquet)

If you need me, I'll be at the hotel Majestic. Goodbye, my love. (she pulls Tommy out)

Saint Franquet (going back)

Now, let's deliver the others. (opens door) Oh!

Bichon's Voice

What?

Saint Franquet

I didn't let you stay in my bedroom to do that!

Plantaredi's Voice

But, since we were together.

Saint Franquet

Never mind.

Bichon (returning, adjusting her dress)

You've got to learn to knock before entering.

Saint Franquet

Enough of that!

Bichon

The things that concern you—with your sister.

Saint Franquet

It wasn't my sister.

Bichon (ironically)

Do you swear it?

Saint Franquet

It was my fiancée!

Bichon and Plantaredi

Huh?

Saint Franquet

Yes, gang, that's how I am. They kick me out. I get married.

Bichon (nervous)

Well, I don't care. What do you want me to do?

Saint Franquet

I know you don't care. Which doesn't prevent me from marrying Miss Dotty Summerson.

Plantaredi

The little American from Chatel-Sancy— My compliments. You won't be sorry. She is charming.

Bichon (furious)

Who asked your advice?

Plantaredi

Huh? No—I said—

Bichon

Yes. Well, if you hurry you can still find her. You can go with her.

Saint Franquet

No.

Bichon

If you're trying to upset me with your marriage! But, I don't give a damn, you know, I don't give a damn.

Saint Franquet

That's exactly what I'm hoping.

Bichon

Still, if you just had a little heart— (tearfully) It's not right, that the very moment I leave you, you go with another—

Saint Franquet

Come on, come on— Don't get excited.

Bichon

Zut! (pulling Plantaredi) Come on, you.

(Doorbell rings.)

Saint Franquet

Hush! Wait!

Bichon

Who cares?

Saint Franquet

No, no. Someone else may be coming to ask for my hand in marriage. Don't budge.

(Saint Franquet goes out.)

Plantaredi

He is funny.

Bichon

You think you're going somewhere with me? Oh, no. One's enough.

Plantaredi

But, what have I done?

Bichon

I don't like tyrants.

(Saint Franquet returns.)

Saint Franquet

Hide one more time.

Bichon

What's going on today?

(Bichon and Plantaredi go into the bedroom. Saint Franquet goes out and returns with Micheline who is carrying a night bag.)

Micheline

Thank God, I found you.

Saint Franquet

I beg you stay in here for a moment. (puts her in bathroom) I have to get everybody out of here. I don't want anyone to see you.

Micheline

Be quick about it!

(She goes in. Saint Franquet locks the door, then opens the bedroom door.)

Saint Franquet

You can come out.

Bichon

Well—finally.

Plantaredi

A woman, huh?

Bichon (to Plantaredi)

If you like, I'll go bring her to you.

Saint Franquet (to Plantaredi)

What do you care?

Plantaredi (slyly)

If Bichon doesn't return tonight, you won't worry.

Saint Franquet

I'd worry if she did.

Bichon

Dirty bastard. Till tomorrow— For my things.

Saint Franquet

That's fine. Go, children.

(Plantaredi and Bichon leave.)

Saint Franquet (opening the door for Micheline)

You! You! In my apartment— But, what brought you?

Micheline (bluntly)

Six months ago, you said if you ever decide to cheat on your husband, let it be with me.

Saint Franquet

Yes, I remember.

Micheline

Well, my friend, the hour has struck. I've decided to cheat on my husband. And here I am.

Saint Franquet (bowled over)

Is it possible?

Micheline

You are happy, thanks.

Saint Franquet

Yes, I am happy. I am very happy.

Micheline

Fine, I haven't wanted it less than you. Tomorrow, you will send your servant to bring my things.

Saint Franquet

Your things?

Micheline

For tonight, I only brought an overnight bag. (she opens it up) Let's see. My nightgown, my slippers—toothbrush—etc. Anything else I think I can find here.

Saint Franquet

But, your things. Why your things?

Micheline

My husband is deceiving me. I can prove it. So, here I am. Take me! I am yours.

Saint Franquet

Huh.

Micheline

I said, "Here I am. Take me, I am yours."

(He falls into a chair.)

Micheline

Is that all the effect this has on you?

Saint Franquet

Listen, Micheline, listen. I am happy. Supremely happy— But— What proof do you have of his infidelity?

Micheline

Proof? I have ten. I have a hundred.

Saint Franquet

Ah!

Micheline

I got a telephone call this morning, from a man who warned my husband to stay away from his girlfriend.

Saint Franquet (aside)

It was you? (aloud) Then what?

Micheline

Well, I had a flea in my ear. I decided to find out. I went through his papers.

Saint Franquet

And?

Micheline

Letters. Lots of letters! (she pulls some out) He got this woman pregnant.

Saint Franquet (astounded)

The bastard! (aside) I'll kill him.

Micheline

It's been going on a long time. And, I'm not going to cheat on him in my turn? Oh—often. I want you to make me pregnant. (she falls into his arms)

Saint Franquet

I haven't the right.

Micheline

Why not?

Saint Franquet

My conscience.

Micheline

You, have a conscience?

Saint Franquet

Yes, I do.

Micheline

Very well. Let's not talk any more. Today I know what your protestations of love are worth. (disgusted) Decidedly, all men are alike!

Saint Franquet

Look—you told me to forget you. That you would never cheat on your husband.

Micheline

That's true.

Saint Franquet

Well, you didn't expect me to run after you all my life— Did you? I was desolated—but today— Well, I'm getting married.

Micheline

Oh!

Saint Franquet

I'm sorry.

Micheline (repacking her bag)

You're quite right. Get married, I will find others. After all, it's better to do it with others.

Saint Franquet

Others? Who?

Micheline

Who? You're not polite to ask.

Saint Franquet

Who? Who are you going to find?

Micheline

There are lots of men who want me. I have an embarrassment of riches in that regard. Des Saugettes, for example.

Saint Franquet

Des Saugettes? He doesn't love you!

Micheline

Doesn't he? He's crazy about me! He'll do anything for me.

Saint Franquet (furious)

The pig!

Micheline

You're not jealous, are you?

Saint Franquet

I am not jealous! I am not jealous! But, that doesn't prevent me from beating him up!

Micheline

Why?

Saint Franquet

Because I don't like to be ridiculous. When I think, you both plan to deceive me.— That this little Jesuit has been playing a game with me.— Ah, fine, I see him.

Des Saugettes (entering)

Ah, there you are— I've just been to the florist.

Saint Franquet (furious)

Do you want me to clean the wall with you?

Des Saugettes (stupefied)

But, my friend—! (seeing Madame Plantaredi) Ah, Madame Plantaredi! (he goes toward her)

Saint Franquet (more fiercely)

Do you want me to clean the place up with you?

Des Saugettes

Yes, yes. (bowing) Goodbye, Madame Plantaredi.

Saint Franquet

My God!

Des Saugettes (fleeing)

Oh, but he's moon-sick.

(Des Saugettes flees.)

Micheline

What's wrong with you now?

Saint Franquet

Him! You!

Micheline

Because I'm going to go to bed with him?

Saint Franquet

Exactly.

Micheline

What do you care? You don't love me?

Saint Franquet

Maybe I don't love you any longer. But—at the moment—I love you. (he pulls her violently against him)

Micheline (pushing away)

Let me go.

Saint Franquet

No—don't be frightened. Why did you resist me, when you did?

Micheline

Because I was an honest woman. Because I didn't cheat on my husband.

Saint Franquet

Well, that was absurd—because you see—now you're going to do it.

Micheline

I wish I had known—but, (shrugging) I didn't.

Saint Franquet

Really? Truly? You don't know how happy that makes me.

Micheline

Why? I'm going to cheat on him—now—but with someone else.

Saint Franquet

We were made for each other.

Micheline (matter-of-factly)

It's too bad. But, you're saving yourself for your wife.

Saint Franquet

I would have loved you so much.

Micheline

Well—it's no use. I no longer have the right.

Saint Franquet

"Right"! A meaningless word when love speaks. When love commands! (pulling her to him)

Micheline (breathlessly)

Are you sure? You don't want to cheat on your wife?

CURTAIN

ACT III

Saint Franquet's bedroom. Door to studio on right. At left, door to bathroom. Windows with curtains tightly drawn. Large bed center.

Knocking on the right. No response.

Des Saugettes (entering)

Gerard! Gerard! You still asleep?

(Saint Franquet snores. Des Saugettes has a bouquet of violets in his hands.)

Des Saugettes

Snoring. Must be still asleep. When he doesn't wake up, he scolds me 'cause I let him sleep. When I wake him up, he scolds me for not letting him sleep. He is so nice!— I'll open the curtains. That way the day will waken him, not me.

(Des Saugettes opens the curtain. No signs of life from Saint Franquet. Des Saugettes coughs.)

Des Saugettes

Hmm! What am I going to do? I will wait till they wake by

themselves. Gerard was in a bad enough temper yesterday.

(Micheline opens her eyes.)

Micheline

Oh! Who opened the curtains?

Des Saugettes (suffocated)

Oh—Madame Plantaredi!

Micheline

Oh. (she hides under the covers)

Saint Franquet (waking)

Huh? What? What's wrong?

Des Saugettes

Oh, Gerard, Gerard!

Saint Franquet

Des Saugettes.

Des Saugettes

You didn't see—there—there in your bed—beside you.

Saint Franquet

What?

Des Saugettes

It's not Bichon! It's Madame Plantaredi!

Saint Franquet (jumping)

What do you say?

Des Saugettes

I assure you, it's she, I recognized her.

Saint Franquet

No, no, it's not true, you hear, it's not true.

Des Saugettes

I tell you, yes! You, you sleep! You don't know! You want to bet?

Saint Franquet

Even if you saw Madame Plantaredi, I repeat—it is not she!

Des Saugettes

Oh—I understand.

Saint Franquet

What do you mean you understand?

Des Saugettes

Nothing. Nothing.

Saint Franquet

Whoever saw such an idiot?

Des Saugettes

Oh—you are still in a bad mood.

Saint Franquet

But, you put me there! What's this business of coming in without knocking?

Des Saugettes

I did knock—but not too loud, for fear of waking you.

Saint Franquet

Did I tell you to come in?

Des Saugettes

No—you were asleep.

Saint Franquet

Then, all you had to do was stay outside. What did you want, anyway?

Des Saugettes

To apologize for what I did yesterday.

Saint Franquet

What did you do, anyway?

Des Saugettes

I have no idea. But you were mad at me, so I suppose I must have done something.

Saint Franquet

No—no— It wasn't your fault— Oh, you make me mad!

Des Saugettes

Now what did I do?

Saint Franquet

Just get out, will you? I can't explain. It's not your fault, but if you hang around much longer, I'm going to kill you.

Des Saugettes

I'm going. (aside) He's sweet.

(Des Saugettes leaves.)

Saint Franquet

He's gone.

Micheline

Much too soon! I thought you were going to keep him here the whole day.

Saint Franquet

I beg your pardon.

Micheline

If you think I was comfortable there— (pointing to the blankets)

Saint Franquet

Poor Micheline.

Micheline (very dignified)

Please call me "Madame."

Saint Franquet (dazed)

Oh!

Micheline

A woman has her reputation to protect.— Really, what's he going to think after this?

Saint Franquet

Nothing at all. What do you expect him to think?

Micheline

Surely, that we slept together.

Saint Franquet

Not at all. I told him that it wasn't you.

Micheline

But, he saw me.

Saint Franquet

Between my word and what he saw, he won't hesitate.— It's a secret that will remain between us.

Micheline

A secret? What secret?

Saint Franquet

This night we spent together.

Micheline

But, we didn't spend the night together.

Saint Franquet (astounded at her audacity)

What?

Micheline

In any case, it doesn't please me to have spent the night with you. There, that's clear. If you had had a little tact—!

Saint Franquet

Oh—I beg your pardon.

Micheline

And, my dear sir, as you have very justly observed that we find ourselves side by side—which is quite incorrect—I ask you to get up.

Saint Franquet

But, I don't want to get up.

Micheline

Good, good. Stay in bed!

Saint Franquet (satisfied)

Ah.

Micheline

You are in your own home. I have nothing to say. (rising) I have to get up. I'll go to the couch.

Saint Franquet (holding her)

No—come here.

Micheline (going to the couch)

You're so gallant. It doesn't surprise me what you did.

Saint Franquet

What? What have I done?

Micheline (on the couch)

When I think, that, but for you— I—a model spouse, who never deceived her husband during six wonderful years of marriage.— No, no. You didn't act like an honest man.

Saint Franquet

That's too much! In what way? In what way?

Micheline

You took advantage of me!

Saint Franquet

How did I do that?

Micheline

You should have convinced me that this was not the right thing to do.

Saint Franquet

You threatened to go to someone else.

Micheline

If you loved me—you should have told me to go, rather than agree to be my avenger— And (sobbing) ruining me!

Saint Franquet

Speaking as a general proposition—saying that to a woman you love is rather hard to do.

Micheline (getting back in bed)

At least you would have had a clean conscience, whereas, now you have my sin on your soul.

Saint Franquet

What are you doing?

Micheline

What?

Saint Franquet

You're getting back in my bed.

Micheline (pushing him out)

Get out. This is not your place.

Saint Franquet

In my bed?

Micheline

In any bed where I am. I am not going to catch cold for you.

Saint Franquet

Good— Good.

(He goes to sit on the chaise lounge.)

Micheline

Oh—you're a nice one— What am I going to do here?

Saint Franquet

That I am asking myself! Because I submitted to your will, you accuse me of a crime.

Micheline

Go ahead. Throw the first stone.

Saint Franquet

Ah, if I had known.

Micheline

Oh, get married, sir, get married. I don't prevent you.

Saint Franquet

Nice to say, after I sent a letter breaking off the engagement.

Micheline

When did you do that?

Saint Franquet

Last night, after we—in a gesture of heroic stupidity—

Micheline

I didn't ask you to do that. Don't pretend you mailed it—

Saint Franquet

No—but, I left it for my servant to do this morning.

Micheline (rising)

Well, ring for him. He can't have done it yet.

Saint Franquet

Yes— I'll do that.

Micheline

At least, you don't try to hide your eagerness to do so from me.

Saint Franquet

Damn it all—

Micheline

And, this is the man who said he wanted to marry me.

(She goes out left.)

Saint Franquet (rings bell)

Victor, come here.

Des Saugettes (enters)

Did you ring?

Saint Franquet

You again? Where's Victor?

Des Saugettes

He left, and asked me to stay till he got back.

Saint Franquet

Did he take the letter?

Des Saugettes

Yes, yes, take it easy. That's why he left.

Saint Franquet

Oh, God! Can you stop him?

Des Saugettes

Why?

Saint Franquet

Because, like a fool, I broke off my marriage.

Des Saugettes

What marriage? You are getting married?

Saint Franquet

Yes.

Des Saugettes

Then, what is going to become of me?

Saint Franquet

Shut up! Who cares! Take a cab and find Victor.

Des Saugettes (ready for action)

Yes.

Saint Franquet

Run—

Des Saugettes

All right. (starts to rush out)

Saint Franquet

Stop!

Des Saugettes (screeches to a halt)

Why?

Saint Franquet

You'll never catch Victor. Go to the Majestic—to Miss Dotty Summerson—

Des Saugettes

Dotty Summerson—Hotel Majestic.

Saint Franquet

Get going.

(Micheline comes in and collides with Des Saugettes, then runs out.)

Des Saugettes

I didn't see her. I didn't see her.

Saint Franquet

Are you going?

Des Saugettes

Yes— (turns back) Hotel?

Saint Franquet

Majestic—

(Des Saugettes disappears.)

Saint Franquet

This seems like a— (opens for Micheline) You were coming to say something to me?

Micheline

It's not true! This seems like a—

Saint Franquet

Curious, I just said the same thing.

Micheline

Ah, you were saying— Charming! Just like your faucets— How come you don't have any hot water?

Saint Franquet

Huh?

Micheline

You only get cold water.

Saint Franquet

I'll fix it.

Micheline

Then, fix it. You know better than I—

Saint Franquet

Just as soon as you asked.

(He goes out. She gets back in bed.)

Micheline

Well, I'm cured of adventures like these. (hearing voices) What's that? There are people in the studio. But they come in and out like a bazaar. (calling) Saint Franquet. (she hides in bed)

Saint Franquet's Voice

Right away.

Micheline

Come, come—oh—

(Bichon and Plantaredi come in, arm in arm.)

Bichon

Cuckoo. Here we are. Gerard! He's not here!

Plantaredi

You believe it will please him, our visit? After all, it's not in very good taste.

Bichon (embracing him)

Oh yes, oh yes— He's a pervert.

(The blanket that hides Micheline gives a little jump when

Plantaredi's Voice is heard.)

Plantaredi

Then, you take it all on yourself?

Bichon

Of course. (calling) Gerard!

Saint Franquet's Voice

It's hot now. I'm coming.

Bichon

What did he say?

Saint Franquet (enters, thinking he is talking to Micheline)

There, there, my dear friend. (seeing Bichon and Plantaredi) Huh?

Bichon

What's wrong with him?

Saint Franquet

Son of a bitch! How did you get in?

Bichon

With my key.

Saint Franquet

What's wrong? What do you want?

Bichon

Why—to pay you a visit.

Saint Franquet

Ah—well—you know.

Bichon

What? It's not nice. Newly married couples visit their families. Well—we consider you one of the family.

Saint Franquet (trying to push them off to the right)

Yes, that's nice of you. Come, this way, this way.

Bichon

But, it's very nice here. You don't have to have manners with us.

Plantaredi (sitting on the bed and taking Bichon on his knees)

Oh, my dear friend—she is charming. Oh, you have taste.

Bichon (coyly)

Oh, sir!

Saint Franquet

Shut up, will you?

Plantaredi

Not at all. I'll speak out. (laughing) My poor wife thinks I am in Chateaudun.

(Movement under the blankets.)

Saint Franquet

Look here, Plantaredi.

Plantaredi (still laughing)

When I came back yesterday, she was out. So I left a message that I had to go to Chateaudun on business.

Saint Franquet (aside)

What an idiot.

Plantaredi

Say—you don't mind my using your telephone to call my wife—from Chateaudun?

Micheline (sitting up in bed)

Oh—you want to telephone me from Chateaudun?

Bichon (frightened)

Ah!

Plantaredi

Son of a bitch! My wife.

(Plantaredi jumps like a rabbit.)

Saint Franquet

Calm down! Calm down!

Micheline

Leave me alone! (to Bichon) Oh! I congratulate you, Madame! You have a nice job.

Bichon

What?

Micheline (to Saint Franquet)

And you, you didn't hesitate to put me in contact with prostitutes.

Bichon (furious)

Prostitutes!

Saint Franquet (to Micheline)

Madame, I beg you—

Bichon

Prostitutes! Which of us looks more like a whore at the moment?

Micheline (indignant)

What do you say?

Bichon

Well, I'm all dressed, and I find you in a nightgown, in my lover's bed—

Micheline

I am an honest woman—and if I am here—it's not for—not for what you pretend to think.

Bichon

No—you're waiting to catch a streetcar.

Micheline

But, to avenge myself! To punish my husband for his infidelities—of which you are the accomplice—to give him as good as I got!

Bichon

Yes? Well, so much the worse for you!

Saint Franquet

Come on, Bichon—enough already. I beg you to shut up.

Bichon

Yes! Well, I beg you to speak differently to me. If you don't like it, my lover is there to answer you.

Saint Franquet

Huh! What lover?

Bichon

Plantaredi!

Micheline

My husband.

Saint Franquet (to Bichon)

You've got a lot of nerve.

Micheline (crying)

Oh—that's all you care for me. That's all you care for me.

Saint Franquet (in despair)

But, what do you want me to do?

Micheline

Oh, I'm a wretch, a wretch!

Saint Franquet

Come on, come on. (to Bichon) Are you happy with your work? I thought you had some heart.

Bichon (softening, to Micheline)

Come, Madame—don't despair. I ask your pardon. I have been too quick.

Micheline (crying)

Ah!

Bichon

Really—I was wrong. Now I understand, you evidently did this after me—because I took your husband.

Micheline (still crying)

Ah!

Bichon

When things like this happen, we don't worry if the guy is married or not. You just can't tell about a John. I suppose we should card them—

Micheline

The wretch!

Bichon

Who? Your husband? No. He's just like all the rest. Only the wife knows or doesn't know. The trouble is, you found out. (to Saint Franquet) Oh, I bet it was you with your idiotic call yesterday.

Micheline (to Saint Franquet)

What? It was you!

Saint Franquet

Yes—

Bichon

Oh—how dumb you can be!

Micheline

Yes—he can be so dumb.

Saint Franquet

Evidently, this is going to be all my fault.

Bichon (to Micheline)

And, why all this? Why are you in bed and why did you—do all that? To revenge yourself?

Micheline

Naturally.

Bichon

It's idiotic.

Micheline

Huh?

Bichon

How have you improved anything? Are you any less deceived today, than you were yesterday? And, did you enjoy it with him? No!

Micheline

No!

Bichon

You see!

Saint Franquet (aside)

Now I understand!

Bichon

Oh—if I'd been there, I'd have warned you— Close your eyes to his faults. Wait for the prodigal child to return. He will.

Micheline

Oh, thanks! Thanks, Madame, for these comforting words.

Saint Franquet (to Bichon)

I didn't know you had these talents.

Bichon

You never took the trouble to talk with me.

Micheline (to Saint Franquet)

There's a woman with a heart.

Plantaredi (to Saint Franquet)

But, it is my wife who is in your bed.

All

Huh?

(Plantaredi goes towards his wife.)

Saint Franquet (interposing)

Plantaredi!

Plantaredi

Shut up!

Micheline

Right! It's my turn to speak.

Plantaredi

No—it's mine. What are you doing here, Madame?

Micheline

Exactly what you were doing last night—I don't know where—at Chateaudun.

Plantaredi

What do you mean?

Micheline

I mean, you were with your mistress— And I, I was with my lover.

Plantaredi

Wretch.

Saint Franquet

It's not true. It's not true.

Bichon

But it's false.

Saint Franquet

Plantaredi, I swear to you.

Micheline

Evidently, that's Mr. Saint Franquet's duty! But me, I affirm it! And, besides, I think the situation is clear enough.

Plantaredi

Very well, Madame. I know what I have to do.

Micheline (rising)

I, too, sir. Fortunately, I have the proofs that will get me a divorce.

Plantaredi

At your ease, Madame.

Micheline

Goodbye, sir.

Plantaredi

Goodbye.

Micheline (with a tender smile to Gerard)

Soon—Gerard.

(Micheline goes into the bathroom.)

Bichon

She's daft— She's gone completely daft.

Plantaredi (to Saint Franquet)

As for you, sir—

Saint Franquet

Fine—cut off further discussion, sir. I owe you satisfaction. I am at your orders.

Plantaredi

Tomorrow—my seconds.

Saint Franquet

That will suffice.

Bichon

If you were not choked up, you would realize this was staged.

Plantaredi

What?

Saint Franquet (to Bichon)

Ah—shut up.

Bichon

No—I will speak. (to Plantaredi) A set-up by your wife, who found out what you did to her, and who decided to pay you back.

Plantaredi

Huh?

Bichon (pointing to Saint Franquet)

And, then, this other dummy—was forced—

Saint Franquet

What?

Bichon

Exactly! Forced to play the role she imposed on him.

Saint Franquet

It's false! It's false.

Bichon

It's false? The proof is (pointing to the bed and the chaise lounge) two beds. Generally, when one give oneself to a man, one doesn't start by making two beds.

Saint Franquet (while Plantaredi listens, stunned)

Oh! Oh! Pardon me!

Bichon

Shut your trap! (to Plantaredi) The real proof is the rage with which they accuse themselves. If you were a psychologist—

Saint Franquet

Will you be finished soon, Bichon?

Bichon

I say you were not the lover of Madame Plantaredi.

Saint Franquet

Yes, I was.

Bichon

No—you weren't.

Saint Franquet

Yes, I was.

Plantaredi (bursting out)

Well, no. You weren't her lover.

Saint Franquet (overwhelmed)

What?

Plantaredi

I tell you, you were not!

Saint Franquet

Plantaredi!

Plantaredi (threatening)

If you don't be quiet—! I can see perfectly clearly. It's clumsy. You can fool me for a while, but not all the time. No—you were not her lover.

Saint Franquet

All right. You win. I wasn't.

Plantaredi

Poor fellow.

Saint Franquet

Old friend.

Bichon (aside)

That took a lot of work.

Plantaredi

I can see it all. Coming to you, mad for revenge. You tried to calm her down— What if she had gone to someone else?

Saint Franquet

I tremble to think of it.

Plantaredi (to Bichon)

You see.

Bichon

Married men are so gullible!

Plantaredi

But, why did she ask for a divorce?

Saint Franquet

It will pass.— But, what she doesn't forgive is your liaison.

Plantaredi

Liaison—? But, just a little folly that started yesterday.

Saint Franquet

She's got your letters.

Plantaredi

I don't have any letters—talk some sense into her. I still love her. Excuse me, Bichon.

Saint Franquet

Go take a walk for a while—Bichon and I—

Plantaredi

Bichon?

Saint Franquet

Bichon has a great influence on her— Let her plead your case, and you will be acquitted.

Plantaredi

My fate is in your hands. (he goes out)

Saint Franquet (opening door)

Come out, Madame, come.

Micheline's Voice

No, no. Hopeless. I don't want to see him.

Saint Franquet

But, he's gone.

Micheline (entering, dressed)

Oh! Where did he go?

Saint Franquet

Who knows? He might blow his brains out.

Bichon

Perhaps throw himself in the river.

Micheline (very calm)

In this weather? No. He hates cold water. Worse luck.

Saint Franquet

What are you going to do?

Micheline

Divorce him. I intend to have my revenge.

Bichon

The best revenge is to send the letters back to the lady who wrote them.

Micheline

No—

Bichon

Really, it would—

Micheline

I don't know, I—

Bichon

Does the woman have a husband?

Micheline

Yes.

Bichon

A husband who knows nothing?

Micheline

Exactly.

Bichon

How's he going to feel?

Micheline

I hadn't thought about that. (after a moment) You are a very chic little woman.— Wait— (she goes out)

Saint Franquet

Where's she going?

Bichon

It worked. She's going to get rid of the letters.

Des Saugettes (comes in, breathless)

Here I am.

Saint Franquet

Ah—you. Did you get there ahead of Victor?

Des Saugettes

No—he got there before me.

Saint Franquet

I told you to take a cab.

Des Saugettes

I did—but I ran into a roadblock—for the President—of the Republic.

Saint Franquet

Damn. Did you see Miss Summerson?

Des Saugettes

Yes. I saw her.

Saint Franquet

What did she say?

Des Saugettes

She said your letter was very funny.

Saint Franquet

Funny?

Des Saugettes

And that it was very silly. And she laughed like crazy.

Bichon

What's all this about? Your marriage is not going well?

Saint Franquet

I wrote her a letter, breaking it off—for reasons I will keep to myself—

Bichon

Which can easily be figured out.

Saint Franquet

I tried to get it back, but this jerk got there too late.

Des Saugettes (indignant)

Jerk!

Micheline (coming with letters)

Here.

Des Saugettes (turning away)

Oh!

All

What?

Des Saugettes

I didn't see. I didn't see.

Micheline

You have convinced me. Here are the letters.

Saint Franquet

To avoid any temptation to change your mind, let's return them immediately.— Des Saugettes.

Des Saugettes (turned away)

I see nothing. Nothing.

Saint Franquet (pulling him around)

You are going to do us a favor.

Des Saugettes

Me? With pleasure. Hello, Madame Plantaredi.

Micheline

Hello, Des Saugettes.

Des Saugettes (to Saint Franquet)

I believe I can now—

(Des Saugettes goes to Micheline and kisses her hand.)

Micheline (very much a woman of the world)

It's been so long since we've seen you.

Des Saugettes

And, Mr. Plantaredi is well?

Micheline (drily)

As well as can be, thanks.

Des Saugettes

Oh—I've forgotten my taxi.

Saint Franquet

That's good. Take it to Madame— (to Micheline) Madame?

Micheline (scornfully)

Madame Chandail.

Des Saugettes

The address?

Micheline

19 Rue Castiglione.

Saint Franquet

That's a stone's throw. Go give this packet to her—if she is alone.

Des Saugettes

Good. (starts to leave)

Saint Franquet

Wait! Tell her this is how an outraged spouse revenges herself.

Des Saugettes

And then?

Saint Franquet

Then, leave. Understand. Hurry!

Des Saugettes

Understood. Au revoir, Madame Plantaredi. (he goes)

Bichon

Feel better?

Micheline

I really don't know.

Saint Franquet

Tomorrow you will thank us.

Micheline

I hope so.

(Plantaredi comes in.)

Micheline

Oh—I will never forgive you.

Saint Franquet

Yes, she will. She's sent the letters back.

Bichon

I got her to do it.

Plantaredi

But, what letters?

Micheline

The letters from Madame Chandail.

Plantaredi

Son of a bitch! Are you all crazy?

All

What?

Plantaredi

Get them back! Get them back.

(Plantaredi goes to the window and opens it.)

Micheline (scared)

Don't do it, Antoine!

Bichon

He's going to kill himself. Help!

(Bichon grabs Plantaredi. The others help.)

Plantaredi

No—no. Get Des Saugettes.

Saint Franquet

He's long gone.

Plantaredi

You've ruined me. Those letters were not mine.

All

Huh?

Plantaredi

They belong to one of my clients.— Son of a bitch. I'll be ruined. Sued for malpractice.

Micheline

How could I possibly know!

Plantaredi (lying down)

My career is ruined.

Micheline

It's not so serious.

Plantaredi

You've given the letters to the adverse party. Not serious! (laughs wildly)

Micheline

It's not the number of letters that's important.

Plantaredi

No. Of course not. But—

Micheline (pulling a letter from her bosom)

This is the most compromising. "My sweetie, you've got me pregnant."

Plantaredi

You've saved me.

Micheline (saintly demure)

I know.

Saint Franquet (to Madame Plantaredi)

You kept it!

Micheline

I'm a woman.

(A knock.)

Victor (enters)

Sir.

Saint Franquet

What is it?

Victor

Miss Summerson.

Saint Franquet

Shit!

Dotty

Can I come in?

Saint Franquet

Certainly.

Dotty

Right. (to Tommy) Wait a minute, Tommy. Oh, you've got everybody here.

(Victor leaves.)

Dotty

Oh—Mr. and Mrs. Chatel-Sancy.

Plantaredi

Indeed.

Dotty (presenting herself)

Miss Summerson.

Plantaredi

We haven't forgotten.

Dotty

How nice. (to Bichon) Oh, Mademoiselle Bichon.

Bichon

Hello!

Dotty (holding Saint Franquet's hand)

Oh—idiot— What a letter you wrote me.

Saint Franquet

Oh—yes—the letter.

Dotty

Funny. What a mess you made.

Saint Franquet

Yes—I guess so.

Dotty

Sending me the letter for Mademoiselle Bichon. (giving it to him)

Saint Franquet (taking the letter to Bichon)

Here, this was for you.

Bichon (reads)

Oh— (laughing) You ass.

Dotty (to Bichon)

Not angry?

Bichon (philosophically)

No, it's life.

Des Saugettes (rushing in)

I did it.

Plantaredi

You sent the letters back?

Des Saugettes (triumphantly)

Yes!

Plantaredi

May the devil take you.

Des Saugettes

Thanks. (to Saint Franquet) Nabbed her just as she was coming out of her house. It was strange— She gave me a kiss. Why did she do that?

CURTAIN

ABOUT THE TRANSLATOR

Frank J. Morlock has written and translated many plays since retiring from the legal profession in 1992. His translations have also appeared on Project Gutenberg, the Alexandre Dumas Père web page, Literature in the Age of Napoléon, Infinite Artistries.com, and Munsey's (formerly Blackmask). In 2006 he received an award from the North American Jules Verne Society for his translations of Verne's plays. He lives and works in México.

www.ingramcontent.com/pod-product-compliance
Lightning Source LLC
Chambersburg PA
CBHW032107090426
42743CB00007B/274